GLOBAL STUDIES

For American Schools

Global Studies

FOR AMERICAN SCHOOLS

by Howard D. Mehlinger
   Harry Hutson
   Victor Smith
   B'Ann Wright

nea

National Education Association
Washington, D.C.

The Authors

Harry Hutson was formerly a staff writer for the Global Studies Project at the Indiana University Social Studies Development Center. In 1978-79 he was the Project Coordinator for the State of Maine, National Inservice Network.

Howard D. Mehlinger is director of the Global Studies Project, director of the Social Studies Development Center, and Professor of History and Education at Indiana University.

Victor A. Smith was formerly a staff writer for the Global Studies Project. He is now Coordinator of Curriculum Research and Evaluation in the Division of Curriculum with the Indiana Department of Public Instruction.

B'Ann Wright was the Associate Director and principal author of the Global Studies Project. She is currently a social studies editor for a textbook publisher.

The Consultants

Bea Barfus, Teacher/Thinking Skills Consultant, Bennett Valley Elementary School, Santa Rosa, California

John Benegar, Social Studies Teacher, Campus Middle Unit, Englewood, Colorado

Jay W. Rinebolt, Chairman, Social Studies Department, Knoch High School, Saxonburg, Pennsylvania

David L. Silvernail, Assistant Professor of Curriculum and Instruction, College of Education, University of Southern Maine, Gorham

Jonathan Swift, Director of Global Education at Stevenson High School, Livonia, Michigan

Library of Congress Cataloging in Publication Data
Main entry under title:

Global studies for American schools.

(Developments in classroom instruction)
Includes bibliographical references.
1. International education.   2. Social sciences—
Study and teaching.   I. Mehlinger, Howard D.   II. Series.
LC1090.G56   300'.7   79-13014
ISBN 0-8106-1824-9

CONTENTS

Acknowledgments

The ideas and sample materials contained in this publication depend heavily upon the work of the Global Studies Project sponsored by the Indiana University Social Studies Development Center. The Global Studies Project, established in 1975, tested the preliminary version of its classroom materials in schools during the 1976-1977 school year.

As members of the Global Studies Project staff, we wish to acknowledge the contributions others have made to the project, especially the contribution of Paul Armstrong, a colleague and an author of one of the six units. We are grateful to those organizations that offered financial support—the U.S. Office of Education through a grant to the Slavic Language and Area Studies Center at Indiana University, the Longview Foundation, and the Social Studies Development Center—and to the many teachers who used the materials with their students and who provided helpful suggestions and criticisms. We also wish to thank Eve Russell for typing the manuscript.

The Global Studies Project is largely dormant now; it no longer has materials for distribution, although there are plans to develop and test revised materials in the future. Thus we are grateful to the National Education Association for providing this opportunity to give the project's ideas greater visibility.

Harry Hutson
Howard Mehlinger
Victor Smith
B'Ann Wright

1. Rationale for Global Studies

We are ruled by concepts. Surrounded by data, we ignore most of it. Objects and ideas gain attention only if they pass through our conceptual filters. These filters—our frame of reference, our perspectives—affect what we see and what we believe about the world.

Concepts are "good" or "bad" according to their utility. Concepts are useful if they discriminate among phenomena and suggest categories that draw attention to important relationships. New conditions prompt new concepts that require new terms to represent them. Carcinogen, nuclear fallout, fluorocarbon, and clone are four relatively new terms that represent concepts that have only recently become important to most of us.

Societies can experience "conceptual lag." Conceptual lag occurs when reality and the concepts employed to describe that reality are out of phase. Sometimes concepts precede reality. The U.S. Declaration of Independence and the French Declaration of the Rights of Man were less a description of the rights most people enjoyed than a prayer for what they hoped to achieve. Nevertheless, the ideas contained in these two documents gave expression to people's strivings and helped shape the future. In other cases the concept can follow reality. The Industrial Revolution had been long underway before it was effectively labeled. And Louis XVI lost his head while still proclaiming the "divine right" of kings.

Today, many Americans seem to be suffering from conceptual

lag when they think about the world. They persist in using conceptual filters called "nation-states," "geographic areas," and "cultural regions." These filters, though useful in the past, do not ease our understanding of a contemporary scene characterized by an ever increasing interdependence of mankind and the accelerating globalization of culture.

Needed: A Global Perspective

During the evolution of social institutions and practices, at what point do people become aware that the accumulation of small changes have produced a fundamental transformation in the society? At what point did enough people depend upon cultivation and animal husbandry to make an agricultural revolution? How many factories existed before there was an Industrial Revolution, and when did labor and management begin to realize their roles in it? When did feudalism give way to nationalism? In short, are people aware of living during eras of massive social change?

Cyril Black believes we are living through a great transformation today. He writes: "The change in human affairs that is taking place [today] is of a scope and intensity that mankind has experienced on only two previous occasions, and its significance cannot be appreciated except in the context of the entire course of world history. The first revolutionary transformation was the emergence of human beings, about a million years ago, after thousands of years of evolution from primitive life. . . . The second great revolutionary transformation in human affairs was that from primitive to civilized societies . . ."[1]

Perhaps Black exaggerates. Nevertheless, it seems evident that a worldwide social transformation is underway. Donald Kendall, chairman of Pepsico, commented succinctly: "The one irrefutable reality in today's world is our growing interdependence; a U.S. failure to recognize this reality would be catastrophic."[2]

What are some of the indicators of this global age? Space permits reference to only a few:

- In 1956 there were 500,000 transatlantic phone calls; in 1975 there were over 24 million such calls.
- International trade among all nations increased tenfold between 1939 and 1969, doubled between 1969 and 1973, and tripled between 1973 and 1977.

9

- Between 15 and 20 percent of all factory workers in the United States are making something for export.
- Nearly half of the oil consumed in the United States is imported.
- About one-third of the profits of American corporations come from their exports and foreign investments. The Ford Motor Company reported that in 1977, 42 percent of its income was from sales outside North America.
- The rate of U.S. investment abroad has grown rapidly—from $1,926 million in 1940 to $3,831 million (1950), $8,009 million (1957), $16,861 million (1964), $29,450 million (1969), and $148,000 million (1977).
- More than 200,000 students from other countries enrolled in U.S. colleges and universities last year. Some universities are now actively recruiting foreign students to fill places left vacant by sagging enrollments of American students.
- In 1900 there were 50 international governmental organizations; today there are 250 such organizations.
- In 1900 there were 60 nongovernmental transnational organizations—e.g., churches, Rotary, unions, business; in 1970 there were 2,300 such organizations.
- Tourism has become a major world industry. Thirty billion dollars was spent on travel last year. Twenty-three million Americans traveled abroad; 18 million people from other countries visited the United States.

"Global interdependence" is more than a glib phrase. It is a fact of life. A sneeze in Hong Kong becomes an epidemic in London and New York; a political decision in Japan creates a bloodbath in Rome or Geneva. The failure of a Soviet satellite raises the possibility of nuclear radiation in Canada; a change in oil production in Saudi Arabia can trigger worldwide inflation and unemployment. Instantaneous global communication via space satellites makes it possible to observe events as they are happening on the other side of the planet. The agenda of world political issues requiring multination cooperation grows steadily.

There has also been a trend toward the "globalization of culture." Norman Cousins described one aspect of this phenomenon a decade ago:

A new musical comedy erupts into success on Broadway and within a matter of weeks its tunes are heard all the way from London to Johannesburg, as though they had pre-existed and were waiting only for a signal from the United States to spring into life. Or a new movie about the Russia of a half-century ago will be made from a book, and all over the world the theme song from *Doctor Zhivago* will be a request favorite of orchestras in far-off places, from Edmonton to Warsaw.

Few things are more startling to Americans abroad than to see youngsters affect the same unconventionalities in dress and manner, whether in Stockholm, Singapore, or Sydney. The young girls with their flashing thighs on Carnaby Street in London or on the Ginza in Tokyo; the young males with their long hair and turtleneck sweaters (with or without beads) in Greenwich Village or the Left Bank or Amsterdam or Hong Kong— all seem to have been fashioned by the same stylist of alienation and assertion.

Or a fashion designer in Paris will decide to use spikes instead of heels on women's shoes, and women across the world will wobble with the same precarious gait. Then, almost as suddenly, the designer will decide to bring women back to earth again, flattening the heels and producing square or wide toes that only a few years earlier would have been regarded as acceptable only for heavy work in the fields—and once again the world's women will conform.[3]

In many aspects of life, there is no longer an "American culture" or "Russian culture" or "Japanese culture." There is a world culture reflected to varying degrees by people in most nations. This has long been true in science, technology, and in the "high culture" of music and art. What is striking today is the extent to which the day-by-day lives of average American citizens show evidence of a transnational culture—movies, music, food, automobiles, appliances, recreation, and so on. And while the importance of language training should not be undersold, more than ever before English has become a universal language.

That Americans understand their own nation—its history and its political and economic institutions—is crucial, but at the same time they should recognize and appreciate the great variations in human culture that exist worldwide. More than ever before, Americans need to develop a species view, a humankind or global perspective, if they are to understand and function effectively in the global society in which they live. Schools, at the elementary through university level, have the primary responsibility for developing this global perspective in youth.

Role of Schools in Global Education

Americans face four major problems in making the transition to a global society: substantive problems, procedural problems, conceptual problems, and value problems.[4]

Substantive Problems

Substantive problems are the stuff of newspaper headlines. They include such topics as the population explosion, energy shortages, the "new economic order" demand of third-world countries, human rights, and the arms race. Americans may differ in how they judge the relative importance of these problems, but few people would argue that they are insignificant or unworthy of investigation in the classroom.

Procedural Problems

Procedural problems focus on approaches to substantive problems. Who will act? Who should be consulted? While everyone readily admits that the gap between rich and poor nations is a serious issue, there is little agreement regarding how to solve the problem or who should solve it. More political battles are fought over procedural questions than substantive ones.

Conceptual Problems

The way any problem is perceived—or whether it is recognized at all—depends upon one's capacity to conceptualize it. Currently, Americans tend to regard food shortages and oil shortages as two distinct classes of problems. The food is ours; we can sell it to whomever we want or even destroy it if we choose (although some people are nearly desperate to get it) in order to keep prices high for farmers. We can use food as a political weapon, making cheap grain available to friends and refusing to sell it to enemies.

But we believe that oil presents a different problem. We don't have enough of it and need more. Our way of life depends upon large supplies of cheap oil. The Arab states have oil; they can't use all they produce, so they should sell what they can't use to us at prices we can afford. Americans generally believe it is unethical for the Arab states to use oil as a political weapon in order to influence our policy toward Israel.

Or consider the way the population problem is conceptualized. The American position is that there are too many babies born each year, so poor nations with high birthrates should enforce strong birth control measures in order to reduce the demand on the world's supply of food and other resources. Third-world nations see the problem differently. The issue, according to these nations, is the gluttonous attitude of the United States and other industrialized nations. One American consumes more of certain world resources in a single year than does an entire Bangladesh village during the same period. There would be plenty of resources to go around, these nations argue, if Americans and other industrialized people would learn to live more modestly. How one conceives the problem makes a difference!

Value Problems

Not only is it important to possess clear and realistic conceptions; the values one holds dear also make a difference. A "conspicuous consumption" attitude has consequences different from those that flow from attitudes of frugality and thrift. People concerned about their neighbors and their children and grandchildren are necessarily different from those concerned solely with themselves and how to make life more comfortable for Number One.

Responsibility of Schools

Teachers have little impact on the immediate outcomes of the substantive and procedural problems described above. This does not mean that such problems should be avoided in classrooms. Nor does it mean that the teacher as citizen should not attempt to influence American policies that bear on these problems. It merely asserts the obvious: a tenth-grade classroom discussion of the population explosion does little to resolve it.

At the heart of education is the impact teachers can have on conceptual and value problems. Teachers as a group have particular opportunities not available to others in American society: they can influence what millions of American youngsters will think and value in a global society. In this way teachers *can* influence how substantive and procedural problems will be handled one day when their current students occupy positions of influence. Unless teachers help youngsters conceptualize human experience in appropriate ways, as adults these students will fail to recognize and solve the problems that will confront them in the future. Educational institutions must always take the lead in understanding the main characteristics of a changing society and in being prepared to consider alternatives for the future. Unless schools can do this, they will merely increase student capacity to predict the past; they will be useless, if not harmful.

Alternative Curricular Responses to Global Education Concerns

There are at least three kinds of curricular responses schools can make to the demand for global education: incorporate a global perspective in all or most existing courses; add units on global issues in some existing courses; develop entirely new courses in global studies. Each approach is summarized below.

Incorporate a Global Perspective in All or Most Existing Courses

No academic discipline or school department owns global education. Helping mathematics students understand the metric system is part of global education. Learning how people in various parts of the world attempt to meet the minimum daily food requirements is a proper topic for health and family nutrition. Music, physical education, science, literature—each subject expands students' understanding of how they have become participants in a world culture. Is soccer a European sport or a game played and enjoyed by youth around the world?

Instruction that could be labeled "global education" has existed for years. For example, modern science is taught largely the same way throughout the world. What is required is that teachers give more emphasis than before to the global dimensions of their subjects. English is a natural partner in global education in the idea that humankind's creativity is universal. Language, writing, literature, humanities—they all express most directly universal anguish, dreams, plans, needs, and joys.

14

Add Units on Global Topics in Some Existing Courses

Students must not only become comfortable with a global perspective, they also need to be exposed to information about global events, issues, and problems. A recent poll of adult Americans found that the majority were unaware of American dependence on foreign oil imports—at a time when nearly 50 percent of the oil consumed in the United States is shipped from abroad, and this dependence is growing steadily. In 1971 a nine-nation study involving 30,000 students and measuring their interest in and knowledge about international affairs showed that American students compared unfavorably when measured against the performances of youth in the Federal Republic of Germany, Finland, Ireland, Israel, Italy, the Netherlands, New Zealand, and Sweden.[5] Simple ignorance is too pervasive. If the United States hopes to function effectively in the world, let alone provide leadership, its citizens need information about world affairs. Units on such topics as food, population, economic development, military security, trade, and international human rights must find their way into existing courses, especially those in the social studies.

Develop Entirely New Courses on Global Studies

There should be opportunities for students to enroll in courses specifically devoted to global studies. Initially these are likely to be elective courses taken by only a few. In time, global studies courses may replace existing required courses as their content proves to be more relevant to the needs of future students. For example, the State Department of Public Instruction in Indiana has recently changed the focus in seventh-grade social studies from "non-Western studies" to "global studies." There are signs that other states are considering similar moves.[6]

Existing courses in world geography, area studies, and world history could easily become more global in their orientation if teachers accepted global education goals. The first step is for teachers themselves to understand the kind of world in which their students will live; then teachers can decide how courses in world geography, area studies, and world history can be revamped to help students cope more successfully with that world.

One Alternative: The Global Studies Project

The Global Studies Project, a curriculum development project of the Social Studies Development Center at Indiana University,

15

was established to provide a global studies alternative to existing world geography and world studies textbooks used in junior high schools. The project developed and tested six units, each requiring an average of five to six weeks of instructional time. Taken together they can be used as a two-semester course. The six units are:

- The Planet Earth in a Global Age
- Families in a Global Age
- Communicating in a Global Age
- Food and Energy in a Global Age
- Working in a Global Age
- Human Rights in a Global Age.

The instructional program rests upon four basic assumptions:

1. *American youth must acquire knowledge, attitudes, and skills that will enhance their capacity to cope with world developments.* The need for Americans to be aware of developments around the world is greater today than in the past and will be even greater in the future.

2. *Eleven- to 13-year-olds are at an optimum age to undertake a serious study of world developments.* Research on the cognitive development of youth suggests that around age 11 children begin to acquire a capacity for formal reasoning and are able to move beyond concrete operational thought. This implies a capacity on the part of children to overcome egocentric perspectives and begin the task of taking into account perspectives different from their own. Because children around this age acquire this ability, i.e., a capacity for role-taking, some scholars believe this to be a "critical period." Opportunities missed at a time when attitudes about other people are being formed can influence responses into adulthood.

3. *It is possible to design instructional materials which treat important social phenomena while anchoring the lessons in areas of interest to young adolescents.*

4. *Studying about the world from a global perspective will help students develop important skills and attitudes more readily than the more typical regional-cultural approach to world geography.*

The last assumption requires further explanation. Most existing junior high school programs in world geography and world studies employ a regional-cultural approach. Typically, students spend several days or weeks studying such nations or cultural regions as India, Japan, Western Europe, Latin America, and the USSR. The students learn discrete facts and information about specific nations or regions but do not learn much about the interconnections, interrelationships, and interdependence of these areas.

It is possible to change the focus—to make the *level* of analysis the entire globe rather than separate geographic areas, to make the *unit* of analysis important human phenomena which are then examined as they exist throughout the world. In this approach students learn less about a specific nation or region, but the stress on comparison and on global relationships helps them develop the knowledge, attitudes, and skills they need to process information acquired later in school or outside of the classroom.

An example might be helpful. There are at least two ways students can learn about food in a world studies program. One approach would focus on the typical food products produced by an individual nation or region, the dietary characteristics of the people who live in that area, and so on. A second approach would explore food production, distribution, and consumption on a global basis. The first approach contributes to an understanding of the culture of a particular area; the second contributes to an understanding of a global process and a pressing world problem.

Until the present, teachers have given little thought to which approach they might adopt. The regional-cultural approach has been dominant. While some educators have pointed to the need for instructional materials featuring a global perspective, to date little has been done to meet this deficiency for the junior high grades. The Global Studies Project attempts to fill this void.

The project developers sought topics of interest to young adolescents, topics that pinpoint important world problems and illustrate interconnections among human beings across national and regional boundaries. A continuing problem has been how to approach global studies in a way that is both interesting and understandable to relatively naive learners. Often the project presents the global topic in terms of experiences typical American youth face each day; in this way the experience is made universal.

To sustain interest, every effort has been made to vary the

17

materials and use a variety of instructional approaches. Case studies, stories, picture essays, and role plays are merely a few types of lessons featured. Many of the lessons depend upon authentic documents and materials gathered from other parts of the world. The project developers also tried to include lessons that strengthen basic skills in reading maps, tables, charts, and graphs.

(NOTE: Most of the activities in this book are intended for students in the middle grades. However, the consultants on the project have emphasized these activities are suitable for students at elementary and secondary levels through creative adaptation by the individual teacher.)

Other Chapters in This Publication

Chapter Two is devoted to sample lessons drawn from each of the six modules that comprised the experimental version of the Global Studies Project. The lessons are written in such a way that they can be adapted for use exactly as they appear. While the lessons are extracted from modules and disengaged from the other lessons that made up an instructional sequence, each lesson can stand alone and should be easily adapted to a great variety of courses. Taken together, these lessons provide a fair sample of the project's work and indicate the type of lessons promoted by advocates of global education.

Chapter Three discusses how the Global Studies Project evaluated its materials. The chapter goes beyond this experience, however, to suggest how teachers can assess what they are doing now in global studies and how they might judge a variety of proposed innovations.

Chapter Four contains some practical suggestions on identifying and evaluating resource materials for global studies.

2. Lessons for Global Studies

The six "lessons" that follow are drawn from the six modules that comprise the Global Studies Project. Each lesson is drawn from a different module. While a few of the lessons involve tasks that can be completed in a single class period, others require two or more days to finish.

Each lesson is organized as follows:

- *Introduction*—states the lesson's theme
- *Objectives*—states what students should be able to do following instruction
- *Suggested procedures*—provides ideas in how to present the lesson
- *Student materials*—the materials to be reproduced and distributed directly to the students. (Teachers must give special attention to how the student materials are distributed. In some cases each student is given a different portion of the student materials.)

Each of the lessons deals with a global concern, although the global ramifications must sometimes be made clear to the students. For example, the first lesson treats how different people wished to use the Great Plains. In a sense this topic concerns only a limited segment of the United States, but the environmental issues raised are global problems.

Since the lessons were drawn from six different units, there is no suggestion that they comprise a sequence of their own. They are merely examples of lessons in global studies, lessons that can stand alone or be adapted for use in many different kinds of courses. Hopefully they may inspire teachers to develop additional global studies lessons.

Lesson I: Who Will Use the Great Plains?

Introduction

One of the most basic global issues today is the relationship between human society and the natural environment. A growing population and an ever higher standard of living put heavy demands on the earth's resources. Thus it becomes increasingly important that students understand how people use and depend on the earth's land, water, and other resources.

In this lesson students learn how a society's culture, values, and technology can influence the interaction between people and environment. They will compare the different ways three groups of people used the resources of one area—the Great Plains.

Objectives

1. Students will be able to compare the impact of three societies on the natural environment of the Great Plains.

2. Students will be able to state how a society's culture, values, and technology can affect the relationship between people and the natural environment.

Suggested Procedures

This lesson could be used in American history, geography, world cultures, or world history courses. It can be used as a role play or as part of a class discussion. Either as part of the lesson itself or as a follow-up activity, students could be asked to research the three societies described or investigate other areas of the world where changing culture, values, or technology is similarly affecting the interaction of people and the environment.

If the lesson is conducted as part of a class discussion, students should read pages 21-26 of the student materials. Use the questions on page 25 to guide the discussion, urging students to consider whether they think the impact on the environment or the contribution to the country's economy is more important. Conclude the discussion with a vote on which of the three groups should use the Great Plains.

If the lesson is done as a role play, ask all students to read the four reports, pages 22-25. Then divide the class into four groups: Indians, cattle ranchers, farmers, and the land commission. Distribute the role cards, pages 27-29, and explain to the Indians, cattle ranchers, and farmers that they will appear individually before the land commission to argue that they alone should have the right to use the Great Plains. Emphasize that each group should discuss the advantages of the land use they support and the disadvantages of the other land uses. The land commission should study the four reports and the questions on page 25 and discuss what factors they think are most important in making their decision.

After the three groups have presented their arguments to the commission, the land commission should vote on which group will be allowed to use the Great Plains for the next 200 years. Lead a class discussion of the results of the role play, noting especially how the values and technology (tools) of the three groups differed. What consideration was most important to the land commission?

Assign the section, "What Happened?", pages 25-26. Ask students whether they think that the oil drillers and coal miners should be able to use the land. What values and tools do they bring to the land? What impact would they have on it?

Student Materials

Imagine that it is 1880, and President Rutherford B. Hayes has appointed a special land commission to plan the future use of the Great Plains. Four reports have been presented to the commission. One report describes the territory and the situation in 1880. The other reports describe three groups of people who want exclusive use of the territory. These reports follow on pages 22-25.

REPORT ON THE GREAT PLAINS IN 1880

The Territory

The Great Plains includes parts of the present-day states of Montana, Wyoming, Colorado, New Mexico, North Dakota, South Dakota, Nebraska, Kansas, Oklahoma, and Texas. It is flat or rolling land with few trees, which usually grow only along rivers or streams. The word "Great" refers to the size of the area: it is 1,600 miles from north to south and averages 400 miles wide.

The climate of the area is continental. Winters are bitterly cold, and summers are hot. The climate is also semi-arid. Most places average less than 20 inches of moisture a year. Another important influence on life on the Plains is the unreliability of moisture. In some years there is plenty of rain or snow, in others there is very little. Drought is a continuous threat.

The Plains are fertile grasslands, home to bison, pronghorn antelopes, jackrabbits, coyotes, and prairie dogs. Large herds of bison, popularly known as buffalo, roamed the Great Plains for hundreds of years before 1880. They adapted well to life on the

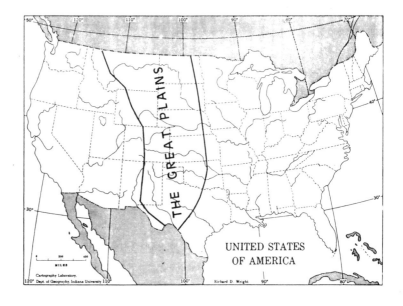

22

Plains. They grew heavy winter coats which they shed during the summer. Furthermore, although bison lived on grass, they could survive without food and water for long periods. By 1880, however, white hunters had killed most bison for their hides.

The Situation

In 1880 cattle ranchers dominate the Plains economy, but farmers from the eastern states are bringing a new way of life to the territory. Only twenty years before, Plains Indians traveled freely over the land. By 1880, however, the Indians have become seriously weakened. The U.S. Army has defeated some tribes, while others have been nearly destroyed by disease. The mass killing of the bison has also threatened the society of Plains Indians.

Representatives of several Indian tribes will appear before the land commission, demanding an end to bison hunting and the return of their land. Cattle ranchers are demanding that farmers stop fencing the land. The ranchers also want the power to decide who can buy land. Farmers want to be able to fence their own land and to buy disputed land, which cattle ranchers use but do not legally own.

REPORT ON THE PLAINS INDIANS

Many tribes of Indians lived on the Great Plains in 1860, among them the Comanche, Dakota, Apache, Arapaho, Cheyenne, and Crow. Most Plains Indians were nomadic people who moved from place to place in search of water and food and did not plow the land to grow crops. Their main sources of food were the wild animals that roamed the Plains, especially the bison.

The bison, which lived on the wild grasses of the Plains, were important in many aspects of Indian life. The bison hunt, for example, was a social event in which young men could show their skill. No more bison were killed than the tribe could use, and no part of the animal was wasted. Extra meat was dried and mixed with berries and roots to preserve it for times when food was scarce. The Plains Indians used bison hide for their clothing, blankets, and tipis, and bison bones were fashioned into buttons, tools, and needles. Even the bison's waste products, usually called buffalo chips, were saved and used for fuel. The Plains Indians used the land but had little impact on it. They moved freely over large areas of the Plains, staying in one place only as long as there was food and water. They seldom disturbed the wild prairie grass, and their limited hunting did not threaten the large bison herds.

REPORT ON THE CATTLE RANCHERS

In 1880 large herds of cattle are grazing on the Great Plains, all the way from Texas to Montana and the Dakota Territory. Twenty years earlier, cattle ranchers began to buy cheap cattle in Texas and drove them north to fatten on the plentiful wild grass. Then cowboys drove the cattle to market in Kansas towns like Abilene and Dodge City. In the 1870s railroads began shipping the fattened cattle east to the big stockyards in Chicago. In 1860 the cattle ranchers shared the Plains with Plains Indians and bison herds, but by 1880 neither the Indians nor the bison are a serious threat.

For the cattle ranchers, at the heart of the issue of land use is the concept of the open range. No one owns the range and there are no fences. Once a cattle rancher is using a portion of the land, however, other cattle ranchers respect his or her right to that territory.

By 1880 the cattle ranchers have replaced the wild bison herds with herds of domestic cattle. Cattle eat the same wild grass as bison, but cowboys can drive them easily to the range and to market.

REPORT ON THE FARMERS

Farmers from east of the Great Plains are beginning to move onto the Plains in 1880, bringing with them a way of life very different from that of the cattle ranchers or Plains Indians. Farmers plow the ground, turning over the soil and any wild plants which grow in it. They then plant crops such as wheat or corn.

Farming has been limited on the Plains until now. The soil is heavy and difficult to plow and there is often a shortage of water for crops. Furthermore, the scarcity of stones and wood has made it difficult to build fences.

Fences are important to farmers because they keep animals from wandering into the fields and trampling the grain. This is a special problem on the Plains where range cattle roam freely. Secondly, fences help establish a farmer's legal claim to the land. A fence around a piece of property tells everyone, "This is my land. Keep off."

Recently farmers have adapted several new inventions that enable them to use the land more effectively. The steel plow easily turns the heavy soil, and windmills pump underground water from deep wells.

However, the use of another invention, barbed wire, has brought the farmer into violent conflict with the cattle rancher. Barbed wire is cheap and makes an effective fence, but as more and more property is marked off by barbed wire, it may mean the end of the open range.

Questions to Consider

1. What impact did the Indians have on the natural environment of the Great Plains?

2. What impact did the ranchers have on the natural environment of the Great Plains?

3. What impact did the farmers have on the natural environment of the Great Plains?

4. Which group had the least impact on the environment of the Plains? Which had the most impact?

5. Which part of the land did each of them use?

6. Which use of the land do you think was most beneficial for the economy of the United States? Why?

What Happened?

The Indians and cattle ranchers eventually lost their struggle. The Indians had been largely defeated before 1880, and afterwards they continued to see their way of life destroyed.

The cattle ranchers' defeat was only partial but was in part a result of their own mistakes. By 1886 too many cattle were grazing on the limited range grass, then in the next years terrible blizzards killed thousands of cattle on the open range. Some cattle ranchers saw the value of fencing in their cattle and feeding them grain during harsh weather. Thus many fenced cattle ranches and feeder lots survived in the Great Plains.

The farmers with their new inventions dominated the Plains in the twentieth century. They plowed and planted more and more land; but like the cattle ranchers before them, the farmers tried to use too much of the land. Many farmers plowed marginal land, and when there were several dry years in the 1920s and early 1930s, the crops died. With no grass or wheat to hold the soil, it began to blow away. During the mid-1930s, part of the Plains was known as the Dust Bowl. Today greater knowledge about farming and better irrigation methods have helped solve some of the problems associated with farming the Plains.

Today another group of people wants to use the land. This group is searching underground for natural resources, especially coal and oil. Oil pumps may have little impact on the land itself, but strip-mining coal from the surface of the land could change the environment greatly—at least while the mine is active. Soil is removed, "stripped" away, until the vein of coal is exposed. The coal is mined, then more soil is removed, and the process continues.

If the land commission were meeting today, would it vote to allow the coal mine owners to use the land? Why do they want to mine the coal? What conditions might the commission set for their use of the land?

ROLE CARD FOR PLAINS INDIANS

You want the land commission to stop the killing of the bison before the herds are completely destroyed. You demand that the cattle ranchers return your land and leave the Great Plains. You also want the commission to stop the movement of farmers onto the Plains. Both groups, in your opinion, destroy the land.

During the debate your group should state how you want to use the Great Plains and why these uses are good ones. You should also state why the uses proposed by the cattle ranchers and farmers are harmful or wasteful.

Use the following questions to prepare your arguments:

1. How do you use the Great Plains? What part of the land do you use?
2. Why is your way of using the Plains less harmful to the

land than the way the cattle ranchers use it? What do they do to the land that you do not? How have they changed the natural environment?

3. Why is your way of using the Great Plains less harmful to the land than the way the farmers want to use it? What will they do to the land that you do not? How will they change the natural environment?

4. How would you defend the charge that your way of using the land does not contribute anything to the country?

5. Why do you think that it is impossible for you to share the Plains with cattle ranchers and farmers?

ROLE CARD FOR CATTLE RANCHERS

You want the land commission to stop farmers from fencing the land. You also think that a board of ranchers should have the right to decide who can buy land within the Great Plains. You believe that the Indians should be controlled by the U.S. Army so they cannot disturb your ranch. You are pleased that the bison herds are almost gone since they could interfere with cattle drives.

During the debate, your group should state how it wants to use the Great Plains and why that use is a good one. You should also state why the uses proposed by the Indians and farmers are harmful or wasteful.

Use the following questions to prepare your arguments:

1. How do you use the Great Plains? What part of the land do you use?

2. Why is your way of using the Plains more important for the United States than the way the Indians used the land? What do you contribute to the country?

3. Why is your way of using the Great Plains less harmful to the land than the way the farmers want to use it? What will they do to the land that you will not?

4. How can you defend taking the land that the Indians formerly used, especially since you did not buy it? How can you defend killing the bison?

5. Why do you think that it is impossible for you to share the Plains with the Indians or farmers?

ROLE CARD FOR FARMERS

You want the land commission to allow you to buy land on the Plains and build fences around your property. You also think that you should be able to buy land which the cattle ranchers have never legally purchased. You are pleased that the Indians are being controlled by the U.S. Army and that the bison herds are no longer a problem.

During the debate your group should state how you want to use the Great Plains and why that use is a good one. You should also state why the uses proposed by the Indians and cattle ranchers are harmful or wasteful.

Use the following questions to prepare your arguments:

1. How do you use the Great Plains? What part of the land do you use?
2. Why is your way of using the Plains more important for the United States than the way the Indians or ranchers use the Plains? What will you contribute to the country?
3. Why are you able to farm on the Plains in 1880 when you could not farm 20 years ago?
4. How can you defend the charge that you are destroying the natural environment of the Plains?
5. Why do you think it is impossible for you to share the Plains with the cattle ranchers and Indians?

ROLE CARD FOR THE LAND COMMISSION

You are a member of the special land commission meeting in 1880 to decide the future of the Great Plains. After hearing arguments from groups of Indians, cattle ranchers, and farmers you must decide which group will be allowed to use the Plains for the next 200 years.

You should also discuss the factors you think are most important in making your decision. There are two main issues to consider:

1. What impact would each group have on the natural environment? Which land use would be the most destructive? Which would be the least destructive?
2. Which group would make the most productive use of the

land? With which group would the land produce enough food to ship out to the rest of the country? Which land use would be most beneficial for the whole country in 1880 and in the following 200 years?

Weigh these two issues and decide whether you think one issue is more important than the other.

Lesson 2: Communicating Across Cultures

Introduction

Communication is often the solution to problems in an increasingly interconnected world, yet communication can also create problems as people from vastly different cultures have more contact with one another. The first two activities in this lesson introduce students to some of the problems created by communicating across cultural barriers—barriers created by entirely different languages and barriers created by jargon within the same language.

The lesson also shows students some of the ways people have learned to communicate in spite of language differences. Many of these communication systems can be considered global languages because they are used and understood throughout the world. Finally, students will use data to analyze the feasibility of designating one language the official global language.

Objectives

1. Students will be able to suggest at least one reason why different languages and jargon can be barriers to good communication.

2. Students will be able to define the concept "global language" and suggest an example.

3. Students will be able to interpret a bar graph and distribution map in order to analyze the question, "Should English be a global language?"

Suggested Procedures

Many students today will already know people who speak a language other than English and will probably realize the problems of communicating across cultures. However, others may never have had such an experience. For those students, you can simulate some of the problems in the classroom.

If possible, obtain from the school language department or local library an audiotape of a foreign language conversation or short story. Tell students that they will hear a short tape, and ask them several easy questions about it. Do not mention beforehand that the tape is in a foreign language.

Play the tape and ask students to answer the questions. Discuss how they felt when they tried to understand the conversation or story. Note that they might have similar feelings if they traveled to a country where they couldn't understand the language. If someone in the class has traveled, she or he might share those experiences. Point out that someone who spoke a language other than English might feel the same way upon hearing an English dialogue.

If you are unable to acquire an audiotape, use a printed excerpt such as the Russian dialogue and its English translation on page 31.

To demonstrate how even one's own language can seem "foreign," ask students to read the material on jargon, page 32. This activity can be expanded by having students investigate jargon used in their own community. Students should prepare a vocabulary list of the jargon and note what each word or phrase means. These lists can be compared in class.

If students have difficulty thinking of an example of jargon, you could suggest some jargon their parents, friends, or other adults might use. The jargon could be related to jobs (factory work, mechanics, law enforcement, teaching, medicine, etc.), sports (bowling, baseball, golf, fishing, tennis, etc.), or other recreation such as television. Even individual families sometimes have their own jargon.

To introduce the activity on global languages, review the definition of a global language: a language that can be understood by persons who normally speak or write different languages. Ask students to read pages 32-34 and suggest examples of global languages in their local community. Then students should read pages 34-36 and study the graph and map. They might work in groups to answer the questions on page 35 in order to prepare an answer to the question: Should English become an official global language? This activity could take the form of a debate.

Student Materials

A RUSSIAN CONVERSATION

В Москве

Туристка. — Извините, гражданин! Вы мне скажете, где Кремль?

Петров. -- С удовольствием скажу. Вы видите там налево огромную площадь? Это Красная площадь. Кремль как раз (just) за площадью.

Т. -- Да, вижу. И это, конечно, Мавзолей Ленина перед стенами.

П. -- Правильно. [Пауза.] Можно спросить, откуда вы?

Т. -- Я с Кавказа, из Баку.

П. -- С Кавказа! Замечательное место! Я был в горах там в прошлом году. Ну, я спешу. Всего хорошего!

Т. -- До свидания и большое спасибо!

In Moscow—

Tourist: Excuse me, sir. Can you tell me where the Kremlin is?

Petrov: I'd be happy to. Do you see that big square there on your left? That's Red Square. The Kremlin is just beyond the square.

Tourist: Yes, I see it. And, of course, that is Lenin's mausoleum in front of the wall.

Petrov: That's right. Could I ask where you're from?

Tourist: I'm from the Caucasus, from Baku.

Petrov: From the Caucasus! What a wonderful place. I was in the mountains there last year. Well, I'm in a hurry. Good luck!

Tourist: Good-bye and thanks a lot!

Questions:

1. Where is the conversation taking place?

2. What is the tourist looking for?
3. Where is she from?

JARGON

Using the same language does not guarantee that you will be able to understand everything you hear or read. All of the phrases in the table below are in English. How many can you understand?

1. point guard set screen high post	3. run a program shut down dump its memory
2. put the hammer down smokey bear 18-wheeler front door	4. come about off the starboard bow tack

The phrases in the first group refer to basketball, and those in the second group are used by drivers with citizens band radios. Computer operators use the phrases in group three, and sailors use the phrases in group four.

Words or phrases that have a special meaning to a group of people are called *jargon*. Jargon can include technical words, but often just gives common words a new meaning. A "high post" literally would be a post that was high, but to basketball fans it means the center is playing in front of the free throw line.

Jargon is used in many occupations, in sports, and in other recreation. Which groups in your community use jargon?

GLOBAL LANGUAGES

Global languages are those that can be understood by persons who normally speak or write different languages. Mathematical symbols, for example, are understood by people all over the world, as are many scientific terms. Some global languages have developed in areas where there has been a long history of contact among people of different cultures.

NaCl means table salt to most chemists no matter what language they speak. Below is an excerpt from a Japanese scientific journal. The explanation is written in Japanese, but the chemical symbols and terms are written in the global language of chemists. This global language is based on a classic language, Latin.

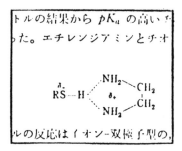

Colors used on physical maps also conform to a global language. In the nineteenth century cartographers from many countries decided which color would be used for water, mountains, and other geographical features. This ensured that everyone could recognize the physical features on a map, even if they could not understand the words printed on it.

New technologies often develop a new language that is understood by anyone who learns to use that technology. Computers do not usually respond to commands in Spanish or Turkish. Many, however, are programmed to understand a language called Fortran that must be learned by their operators.

Even if you are not a computer operator, a scientist, or a mathematician, you will probably read a global language sometime in your lifetime. One such language is already being seen in the world's airports and on its highways and attempts to overcome communication problems by using pictures and nonverbal

symbols to relay the message. On the previous page are several examples of the global language of international travel. What do they mean? Have you seen any examples of this global language in your community?

SHOULD ENGLISH BE A GLOBAL LANGUAGE?

Picture symbols are fine for international travelers, because only a small amount of information is needed. Chemical symbols work for chemists. But if you want to become friends with people or do business with them, you have to be able to write or speak a more complex language.

Today people can contact any part of the world in seconds, and they can travel there in hours. They need a language they can use everywhere, but so far no such language exists.

Attempts have been made to construct a global language. One of the more successful has been Esperanto, a language invented in 1887. Today 100,000 people in 83 countries use Esperanto,

Language Use

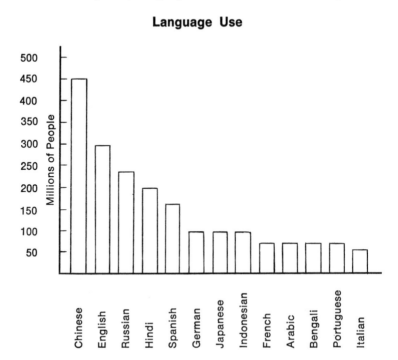

but no country or international body has accepted Esperanto as an official language.

Some people have suggested that English is becoming a truly global language, especially as an increasing number of the world's political and economic leaders use it. Carefully study the bar graph on the previous page and the map that follows, and consider the arguments on page 36. Based on this information, do you think English should become an official global language?

What does the bar graph show you? Which languages are used by over 150 million speakers? How many speakers does each of those have? Which language is spoken by the largest number of people?

The map at the bottom of this page shows the distribution by country of the five most widely used languages. Countries in which the language is either official or widely used are shaded. Which language is used in the most countries? Which language has the widest geographical distribution?

Should English become an official global language? Why or why not?

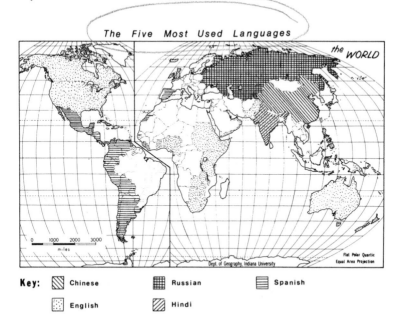

The Five Most Used Languages

the WORLD

0 1000 2000 3000
miles

Flat Polar Quartic
Equal Area Projection

Dept. of Geography, Indiana University

Key: Chinese   Russian   Spanish
         English   Hindi

Arguments in favor of the proposal:

1. English is spoken by one of every seven people on Earth.
2. A large number of people learn English as a foreign language. There are 50 million students of English in the Soviet Union. It is the main foreign language taught in France and Germany, and in Swedish schools English is a required subject from the fourth to seventh grade.
3. English is already widely used in science and international business.

Arguments against the proposal:

1. Six of every seven people on Earth do not speak English.
2. English is a difficult language to learn.
3. English, as the official global language, would threaten the survival of many rich and beautiful cultures around the world. Language is a very important part of culture, and if people lose their language it would be very easy for them to lose part of their culture.
4. There could be political problems if English were the official global language. English is the official language of the United States of America, and its political rivals would oppose the selection of English. Some nations might fear political or economic control by the United States if English were the official global language.

Lesson 3: A Dilemma of Modern Industry

Introduction

Modern industrial plants are characteristic of a global society. Raw materials and finished products flow continuously from one nation to another. As industrialization spreads, ever more people become involved in this process, either by using the products made in factories, working in factories, or living nearby.

Through this lesson students will begin to appreciate one way that industrialization can affect people's lives, including their own. The lesson will also introduce students to one of the difficult dilemmas of modern industry—the same factories that provide employment and economic well-being to a community may also threaten its health.

Objectives

1. Students will be able to assume the role of a participant in a controversy over industrial pollution and will be able to defend their position.

2. Students will be able to describe both sides of the dilemma presented in the role play.

Suggested Procedures

Assign pages 37-38 as background reading. Then divide the class into five groups for role play:

1. Stop Gorkon
2. Safety First
3. Gorkon Officials
4. All for Stoddard
5. City Health and Safety Committee (CHSC)

Each group should read "The Situation" on pages 38-39 and study its role as described on pages 39-40. The "witness" groups should prepare the arguments they will use during the hearing, and the CHSC should discuss the criteria it will use to make its decision.

Conduct the hearings by allowing each group two or three minutes to present its arguments. The groups should also respond to questions from the CHSC. The CHSC should then prepare written answers to the questions on page 40, including an explanation of the consequences of each action.

After the CHSC presents its report to the class, lead a class discussion of the results. Students should express their own opinions during this discussion. Possible questions include: Why do you think the CHSC reached the decision it did? Was the decision realistic? Why or why not?

Ask students to read the section, "Modern Disasters," pages 41-42, and compare these situations with the one they simulated. They should also discuss any similar situations that may have developed locally. These could be chemical spills into waterways or the air as well as other forms of pollution.

Student Materials

Although it has solved many problems and has made life easier for many people, the development of modern industry has had dangerous side effects for both the people who work in the factories and for the surrounding community. This fact has been evident since the earliest industry in Great Britain, although the specific dangers have changed over time. Early factories in the United States and in Europe were often dark, dirty, and dangerous places in which to work. Plant accidents killed and crippled workers because machinery had few safeguards to protect workers from accidents.

Industries also polluted the air and water around them. Coal was the main air polluter; it powered industry for over 100 years and is still used widely today. Much coal has a high sulphur content and burning it creates sulphur dioxide and other gases that can irritate and damage lungs. Waste products from industries and from the growing population of cities have clogged rivers and destroyed the plants and animals that lived in them.

Some of the early industrial dangers are of less concern today. In most nations with a high level of industry, the physical working conditions in factories have improved greatly during the past century. Safety equipment and strict factory rules have reduced the types of accidents that were once common.

Some important advances have also been made in controlling air and water pollution. However, pollution is still a major problem. As modern industry spreads around the globe, so does the threat of pollution.

While the battle for plant safety and against pollution continues, we have discovered a new danger to workers and the public. During the past thirty or forty years, scientists have created thousands of new chemicals widely used in industry. Many of these chemicals are extremely dangerous to humans, although in some cases they have been used for as long as twenty years before the danger was discovered. Some familiar substances have also been shown to have harmful effects. In the role play described on the following pages you will explore the dilemma created by these developments.

OMICRON II

The Situation

Imagine that the year is 2174. Five years ago Gorkon Products opened a plant near the town of Stoddard to manufacture seats for electric automobiles, the only kind still used on Earth. From

2165 to 2169, few cars were made because there was a severe shortage of the material used to make car seats. Then in 2169 Gorkon Products discovered Omicron ɪɪ, a product both inexpensive to produce and very durable. New seats made of Omicron ɪɪ were rushed into production, and the people of Earth were relieved.

But in 2174 there was disturbing news from Stoddard. Several workers were taken to the hospital because they had trouble breathing and were experiencing uncontrollable shaking. A week later more workers became ill and so did some members of their families. By the end of the month 75 Gorkon workers were in the hospital. The crisis worsened when nearly 50 local citizens also became ill with the shakes.

Doctors and health officials worked 24 hours a day to find the cause of the illness. In the meantime five people died, although other patients improved enough to leave the hospital. Finally, doctors found traces of Omicron ɪɪ in the blood of nearly all victims of the disease. They have not yet been able to prove that Omicron ɪɪ caused the shakes, but they have urged Gorkon Products to stop using the substance. Some Stoddard citizens are also demanding that the Gorkon Products plant be closed.

The Stoddard City Council has asked the City Health and Safety Committee (CHSC) to decide what should be done. The decision is an important one for Gorkon Products and for the citizens of Stoddard for several reasons. First, people's health and even their lives appear to be in danger. However, Gorkon employs nearly one-third of the townspeople of Stoddard, and if the plant is forced to close, many people will lose their jobs.

The decision is important for the world as well. Only Gorkon makes car seats, and there is no substitute for Omicron ɪɪ. If the CHSC decides to shut down the Gorkon plant in Stoddard, other Gorkon plants will probably be forced to close. Since no car seats could be manufactured, electric car production would stop. Thus the world watches and listens as the CHSC hearings open.

Witnesses

Four groups of witnesses will plead their cases at the CHSC hearings:

1. "Stop Gorkon" is a group of workers and citizens, many of whom are ill. Its most outspoken members are relatives

of the persons who died. "Stop Gorkon" demands that Gorkon pay each victim of Omicron II between $75,000 and $200,000 for the losses he or she has suffered. The group also demands that the Gorkon Products plant be closed at once.

2. "Safety First" is a citizen's group that has promoted industrial safety for many years. They propose a far-reaching safety program that would make it safe to manufacture car seats from Omicron II. This program would include installing a series of dense filters in the plants' smoke stacks, providing protective clothing and masks for workers, and offering constant medical supervision of employees.

3. Gorkon officials argue that it has not been proved that Omicron II caused the illness in Stoddard. If Omicron II was responsible, they claim, people were probably exposed to the substance because of carelessness by a few workers. Officials agree that the matter should be investigated, but they feel that new and expensive safety measures are unnecessary. Some officials predict that the high costs of payments to patients and special safety equipment could force Gorkon to close. Besides, they note, Omicron II is vital in the production of cars.

4. "All for Stoddard" is a group of businesspersons and Gorkon workers who argue that the Gorkon Products plant must be kept open. Shutting down the plant would lead to a serious loss of jobs and a drastic reduction of income to local businesses. They feel that the danger of illness has been exaggerated; they say only a small percentage of people have become ill.

City Health and Safety Committee

The CHSC must listen to the arguments of the four groups and then decide three important questions:

1. Should Gorkon Products be required to make payments to persons who suffer from the shakes? (If so, how large should the payment be?)
2. Should Gorkon Products be required to install new safety devices to protect workers and the public from Omicron II?
3. Should Gorkon Products be required to stop using Omicron II?

During their meeting, the CHSC must consider what could happen if they voted "yes" on a question, and what could happen if they voted "no." When the hearing is completed, the CHSC will prepare a report for the City Council stating their conclusions and the reasons for their decisions.

Modern Disasters

The Omicron II case is fictional, but it is based on actual situations. The details differ, but the basic problem is similar: some industries can be dangerous to human health, but controlling this danger may mean a loss of jobs and income.

One real-life industrial disaster took place in Minamata, Japan. During the 1950s people in Minamata began to fall ill; many were crippled and suffered brain damage. Several years later doctors discovered that the symptoms were caused by mercury poisoning. Chisso Corporation, a large chemical factory, had for years dumped its waste into Minamata Bay. The mercury came from Chisso waste. Fish from the Bay were a staple in the diet of Minamata citizens, and people acquired the mercury from eating the fish.

The population of the Japanese town was badly split over what should be done. In 1969 one group of patients sued the company, demanding that Chisso pay them for their injuries. During the trial they held sit-ins and hunger strikes to draw attention to their cause. Another group of people supported Chisso because so many people relied on the company for their livelihood. This group claimed, "They [the victims] ate weak fish and got sick because they felt like it." In 1973 the victims of mercury poisoning won their suit. Chisso had to pay each victim between $60,000 and $68,000. The total amount paid out was more than $80 million.

In recent years we have become aware of other industrial threats to health. For example, on July 24, 1975 the Virginia Board of Health closed a plant in Hopewell, Virginia. For 16 months the plant had been producing a product called Kepone, a pesticide used to kill insects both in the United States and in other parts of the world. The plant was ordered closed when almost half of the 150 workers became ill from the poison. The symptoms of the poisoning included shaking, slurring of speech, damage to the liver, and pain in the chest and joints. The danger spread beyond the plant workers, however. Their families were affected because the pesticide clung to the work clothes they wore home. In addition, waste from the plant flowed into the James River, a major fishing area. In December 1975, Governor Godwin closed the river for fishing.

Summing Up

How are the modern disasters discussed above similar to what happened in the Omicron II simulation? How are they different?

If an important industry in your community were polluting the air and water, what would you do? What would you do if you worked for the industry?

Lesson 4: Changing Energy Needs

Introduction

A growing world population is putting pressure on food and energy supplies. Contributing to this pressure is the spread of modern farming techniques and increased industrialization in all parts of the world. Both require large amounts of nonrenewable fossil fuels. In this lesson students will interpret circle and line graphs to see how world energy use is changing. The lesson can be expanded by asking students to research other possible energy sources: nuclear energy, solar energy, wind power, methane gas, thermonuclear fusion, geothermal energy, thermocline energy, or tidal energy.

Objectives

1. Students will be able to define "renewable energy source" and suggest examples.

2. Students will be able to define "fossil fuel" and suggest examples.

3. Students will be able to read and interpret circle graphs in order to analyze changes in energy use over time.

4. Students will be able to suggest reasons why the worldwide use of fossil fuels is increasing rapidly.

Procedures

After students have read pages 43-45 as background, review the definition of a renewable energy source and ask students whether they use renewable fuels in their everyday lives.

42

Ask students to study the circle graphs on page 44 and answer the questions that follow. Students should see that the most widely used fuel in the U.S. has changed over the years. They can trace the decline of wood, the rise and decline of coal, and the rise of oil and natural gas by comparing the appropriate portions of each circle.

The graph on page 46 illustrates the increased worldwide consumption of fossil fuels. Consumption is measured in quadrillion BTUs, but students do not have to concern themselves with this unit of measurement. The change in the raw numbers from approximately 120 to approximately 340 is ample evidence of the growth in consumption.

The top line of the graph represents the total world consumption of coal, petroleum (oil), and natural gas. (Nuclear and hydroelectric power are not included in the graph.) The percentage figures show what proportion of *all* fuels consumed was natural gas, petroleum (oil), and coal. For example, in 1960, 34 percent of all fuel consumed was oil. Ask students to note how the proportion of each fossil fuel is expected to change from 1960 to 1990. Conclude with a class discussion of the questions on pages 45-46.

Student Materials

At one time people all over the world relied largely on sunlight and wood as sources of fuel for heating, cooking, and light. Both sunlight and wood are renewable energy sources—ones that reappear or can be created again. A third traditional fuel, animal waste, is also renewable.

Long before today's interest in solar energy, some groups of people developed sophisticated ways to make the most of sunlight for heating. Over 1,000 years ago Indian cliff dwellers in what is now Colorado built their dwellings so that they could use heat from the sun to keep warm in the winter. The cliff dwellings at Mese Verde face south so the winter sun, which is low in the sky, shines directly into them. During the day heat from the sun is absorbed by the dark rear walls of the dwellings. Then during the cold nights the walls release the heat, warming the homes. In summer, the sun is high in the sky and shines down on the roofs of the dwellings. The roofs reflect the sunlight and the insides of the dwellings remain cool.

Today, one-third of the world's people still depend on wood

for heating and cooking. Although wood is a renewable resource, trees grow slowly. The increasing demand for wood means that new trees cannot grow fast enough to replace those cut down.

In India and Bangladesh, for example, so many people need firewood that trees have become scarce. People often spend the entire day searching for enough wood to meet their families' needs. The Indian government has tried to plant trees for future use, but such attempts have largely failed. The need for firewood is so great that trees are often cut down before they are fully grown.

In Nigeria, where wood is a major fuel, the destruction of the forests presents another related problem. As people cut down more and more trees, there is no vegetation left to hold the soil

A Shifting Demand

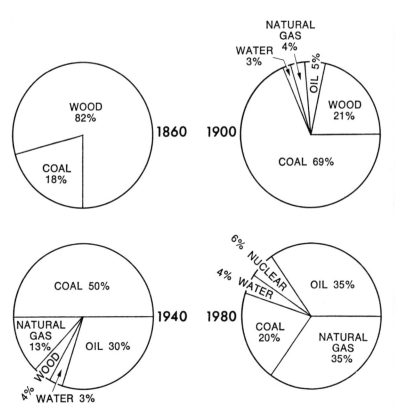

in place. When it rains, the fertile topsoil washes away, and forests and farmland gradually change into desert, leaving less land suitable for growing crops or trees.

Both sunlight and wood continue to be important sources of energy; however, over the past 200 years human society has turned increasingly to other types of fuels. The circle graphs on the previous page illustrate how energy use has been changing in the United States.

Based on these graphs, what was the major type of energy used in the United States in 1860? in 1900? in 1940? What fuel was used widely in 1860 but hardly at all in 1940? What fuel not used in 1940 will be used in 1980?

The graphs show a trend in energy use in the United States from wood to fossil fuels. Fossil fuels—including coal, oil, and natural gas—are formed from dead plants which have decayed under intense heat and pressure for thousands of years. This process takes so long to complete that fossil fuels can be considered nonrenewable. Once they are used, they can never be replaced. Nevertheless, fossil fuels have replaced wood for several reasons: there is more available; they are easier to use; and they can be used for a variety of purposes.

Coal was first used on a wide scale in Great Britain in the 1700s. Much of the industry which developed in Western Europe and in the United States in the 1800s was powered by coal. As you can see on the graphs, oil and natural gas were little used in the U.S. in 1900, but their use has grown rapidly since then. As countries like the Soviet Union and Japan developed modern industry, they too have used increasing amounts of fossil fuels. Today the spread of industry and modern farming methods to Latin America, Africa, and Asia means that those areas will also increase their dependence on fossil fuels.

The graph on the next page shows the rapid growth of the world's total use of fossil fuels from 1960 to 1990. (Figures beyond 1974 are estimates.)

Examine the graph and use the information to answer the following questions:

1. How much fossil fuel was used in the world in 1960? How much will probably be used in 1990?

2. According to the graph, consumption of which fuel is expected to grow the most between 1960 and 1990?

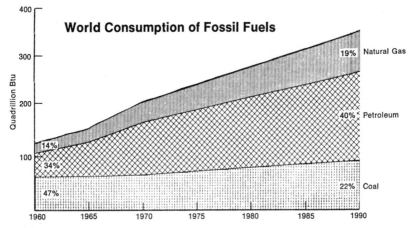

Adapted from: *Energy Facts II,* U.S. Government Printing Office, 1975.

3. The percentages on the graph indicate each fuel's proportion of total fuel used; thus, in 1960, 34 percent of all fuel used was petroleum. Consumption of which fuel is expected to show the greatest proportionate increase between 1960 and 1990? Which is expected to show a proportionate decline? Is this consistent with what you learned about the change in energy use in the United States?
4. Why do you think modern farming requires a greater use of fossil fuels than traditional farming? What is the source of energy in each case?
5. The graph illustrates the growing use of three major fossil fuels. What other sources of energy might become increasingly important in the future?

Lesson 5: Picking Partners

Introduction

It is extremely important to understand the intent of this lesson before presenting it. The purpose of the lesson is to understand *alternative lifestyles, not to attach a particular value to them.*

American students are brought up in a culture that thinks, talks, and sings about "falling in love," and they have difficulty comprehending a system of arranged marriage, where love grows after the wedding instead of before. A comparison of arranged

46

marriages and love marriages is the subject of this lesson.

Students will analyze advertisements from a New Delhi news-paper as evidence of modern arranged marriages, and they will discuss two case studies representing variations in this custom. They will also read a fictional conversation between an Indian and American student that summarizes some advantages and disadvantages of arranged and love marriages.

Objectives

1. Students will be able to define and give examples of ar-ranged and love marriages.

2. Students will be able to compare the patterns of arranged marriage in India and Japan.

3. Students will be able to list advantages and disadvantages of both arranged and love marriages.

Suggested Procedures

Ask students to study the classified ads reproduced on page 49, then pose the following questions:

1. What is the purpose of this page?
2. Where is it from?
3. Who is advertising for marriage partners?
   a. Men or women? (both)
   b. Rich or poor? (rich)
   c. Educated or uneducated? (educated)
   d. City dwellers or rural villagers? (urbanites)
4. What requirements are listed for marriage partners?
5. What seems to be important about marriage according to the ads? Caste? Education? Appearance? Wealth? Social status?
6. Have you ever seen ads like this in American newspapers?

The following definitions may help you answer questions students might have about the matrimonial advertisements:

Brahmin—the highest caste in India

castes—community groups in India formed originally around occupations

"Caste no bar"—intercaste marriage is a possibility

dowry—a gift of money or goods given by the bride's family to the bridegroom and his family

47

homely—interested and skilled in homemaking

Jain—a religious minority comprising 0.5 percent of the population

rupee—Indian currency, worth about 12¢ (January 1975 rate)

Sikh—a religious minority comprising 2 percent of the population

After discussing the matrimonials, ask students to read pages 50-51, especially noting the definitions of "love marriage" and "arranged marriage." Two examples of arranged marriage follow, one from India and one from Japan. Students should read each story and compare the cases using the questions on page 53 as a guide.

The reasons behind a system of arranged marriage are explored in the dialogue entitled "A Conversation on Marriage." You might ask two students to read the parts of Heather and Radhika in front of the class. After reading the dialogue, discuss the questions on page 55-56, paying particular attention to cultural differences. Question 2 may speak to the concerns many students have about their personal appearance. Discuss why "looking just right" is important in American teen-age society. Countless products advertised on television cater to this concern: cosmetics, deodorants, mouthwash, clothing, various status symbols such as certain automobiles. Even some toothpastes claim to impart sex appeal.

An optional activity which might be interesting to your class would be a debate on the topic, "Resolved: A System of Arranged Marriages Promotes a Society with Fewer Anxieties and More Stable Families." The data in the dialogue can generate ideas for the debaters.

Student Materials

On page 49 is a section of advertisements called "matrimonials" from the August 11, 1974 edition of the *Hindustan Times*. This English language newspaper is published in New Delhi, the capital of India.

This kind of advertising may seem strange to you. Not too many years ago, it would have seemed strange in India also. Advertisements for mates have become popular only within the last 20 years, in large cities where it is difficult to find eligible

Jabl Nanda boy, well settled in USA, own business. Contact Box 20561-CA/R, Hindustan Times, New Delhi-1.

WANTED suitable bride for 27 years old Punjabi Flying Officer. Early marriage. Contact Box 20560-CA,R, Hindustan Times, New Delhi-1.

BRAHMIN match for 29 yrs., Sales Rep. D.C.M., getting 600/- P.M. Box 21001-CA. Hindustan Times, New Delhi-1.

MATCH for handsome Gaur Brahmin Bharadwaj Graduate boy, age 26, private service, pay Rs 400/-. Box 21019-CA, Hindustan Times, New Delhi-1.

BOMBAY settled Khatri, 26, Engineer, 173 cms., salary 2000/- P.M. with perks, seeks accomplished bride. No bars. Box 20902-CA, Hindustan Times, New Delhi-1.

MULTANI beautiful match preferably Govt. employee for hansome, 25 Railway service. B-9/6708, Dev Ngr., New Delhi. 20905-CA

WANTED tall, accomplished domestic girl for 28 years, fair complexioned, 177 cms., Kapur bachelor from Delhi, only son with landed property, monthly four figure income. No demand except good girl. Box 20908-CA, Hindustan Times, New Delhi-1.

SUITABLE match for Arora boy, 27, well settled in business. Income four figures. Family residing in Delhi and Muzaffarpur. Early marriage. Box 20964-CA, Hindustan Times, New Delhi-1.

WANTED a bride preferably Medico for a handsome Doctor Kayastha bachelor, 25, 173 cm., doing M.D. Box 20966-CA, Hindustan Times, New Delhi-1.

GIRL Dr./M.A. English or Science for Hindu boy, about 34, highly educated Lecturer College of Technology, London. Girl to accompany U.K. by mid-September, Caste no bar. Contact Mr. Bhatia, B-2/66, Safdarjung Enclave. Tel. No. 70828.   20912-CA

A TALL, graceful, convent educated Sanadhya Gaur Brahmin girl for a young man of 25, drawing Rs. 1,000/- p.m. H.U.F. income nearly Rs. 50,000/- p.a. Write:— Mr. Singh, Surajpur House, Mathura Road, Agra-2.   62623-M

WANTED beautiful, educated match around 20-22 for handsome Bisa Agrawal bachelor, 27, Engineer, owning industry, belonging educated, cultured and respectable well connected family. Box 63338-CH, Hindustan Times, New Delhi-1.

MATCH for handsome Kanyakubja Brahmin boy, 27, 165 cms., Post-graduate, decently employed in New Delhi. Sub-caste no bar. Box 20842-CA Hindustan Times, New Delhi-1.

SUITABLE match for a Khatri boy, 29, Ph.D. (Physics) from USA shortly returning India. Lecturer/PGT preferred. No bars. Box 20899-CA, Hindustan Times, New Delhi-1.

SUITABLE match for Khatri Electrical Engineer, 28, Manager local factory, drawing 1400/-. Locally employed, teachress preferred. Box 20916-CA, Hindustan Times, New Delhi-1.

ARORA businessman earning four figures, 28 yrs. needs homely, good looking, cultured life companion. Box 20929-CA, Hindustan Times, New Delhi-1.

MATCH for a Punjabi Arora boy, age 26, Conductor in D.T.C. Box 20941-CA, Hindustan Times, New Delhi-1.

EMPLOYED match for Gursikh Lecturer boy, Delhi University, 28, Rs. 1050/-, own house. Send full particulars. Box 20950-CA, Hindustan Times, New Delhi-1.

WANTED match for Punjabi Brahmin Engineering Graduate, 29, settled in U.S.A. $1000 per month, Box 20959-CA, Hindustan Times, New Delhi-1.

BRAHMIN match for Engineer, 27, owns property in New Delhi and nearby. Income in four figures. Girl should be beautiful and from family of status, Box 20952-CA, Hin-

cialist 32, emoluments 1500/-, Box 21081-CA, Hindustan Times, New Delhi-1.

WANTED beautiful preferably convent educated girl for young handsome Khatri qualified Ground Engineer (IAF) 27 with income in four figures and bright future prospects. Box 21074-CA, Hindustan Times New Delhi-1.

BEAUTIFUL bride preferably convent educated fo- handsome Graduate boy, 25, in his own lucrative business, belonging to reputed local Aggarwal family. Box 21069-CA Hindustan Times, New Delhi-1.

PRETTY girl for handsome well educated Punjabi young boy 25, earning high four figures in well established high class business. Early marriage. Ring 387129. Apply Box 21068-CA Hindustan Times, New Delhi-1.

FOR SIKH Arora boy, 24, undergraduate having Iron Steel Hardware Machinery industrial business, local branches, sole proprietor, owns property, homely beautiful girl from respectable family only. Box 21053-CA, Hindustan Times, New Delhi-1.

AHLUWALIA match for my only son, Graduate, 27 yrs., (5'-9") 172 cm., owns business. Box 20778-CA, Hindustan Times, New Delhi-1.

BEAUTIFUL Shrivastava, Medico girl for handsome, tall, B.Sc., M.B.B.S. Doctor, aged twenty-six years in Govt. service. Apply Box 20779-CA, Hindustan Times New Delhi-1.

RAJPUT match for a Raghuvanshi (Bhardwaj) boy 26, 5'-6" (169 cms.), studying M.Com., Govt. service, drawing over Rs. 600/- P.M. Father's income four figures. Girl's merits only consideration. Please apply with full particulars. Box 20527-CA/R, Hindustan Times, New Delhi-1.

HOMELY, respectable bride for Punjabi, Khatri, M.Sc. boy, 28, Government employee salary Rs. 1000/-. Apply B1/53/1, Safdarjang Enclave, New Delhi-16.   20787-CA

WANTED preferably Medico match for 28, handsome Ahluwalia boy, M.B.B.S. flourishing practice South Delhi. Father Senior Govt. Officer. Caste no bar. Box 20794-CA Hindustan Times, New Delhi-1.

BEAUTIFUL, tall, educated for Agrawal bachelor, 30, Physics Lecturer. Box 20797 CA, Hindustan Times New Delhi-1.

BEAUTIFUL Medico match for handsome, 28 years, Punjabi speaking Bansal Agarwal, M.S. boy, belonging to well settled family in Delhi. Box 20692-CA, Hindustan Times, New Delhi-1.

BEAUTIFUL, employed girl for Punjabi, Khatri boy, 29 yrs., 170 cms., Diploma Civil Engg., Govt. service, getting Rs. 600/-. Box 20721-CA, Hindustan Times, New Delhi-1.

TALL, beautiful, locally employed match for handsome young, Punabi Brahmin bachelor, 33, Central Govt. service, drawing 825/-. Caste no bar. Box 20736-CA, Hindustan Times, New Delhi-1.

PROFESSIONALLY qualified lady for handsome sophisticated Brahmin, from West U.P. Professor in renowned American University, PH.D., from top varsity 35, visiting India. Absolutely no bar. Box 20737-CA Hindustan Times, New Delhi-1.

WANTED Teachress or working girl for Khatri Graduate, 26 yrs., serving Voltas, Rs. 860/-. Apply Box 20741-CA, Hindustan Times, New Delhi-1.

BRIGHT match for Graduate Arora boy, 27, working with Air Line, Delhi, preferably Teachress, respectable family. Apply Box 21126-CA, Hindustan Times, New Delhi-1.

PREFERABLY Teacher for Arora boy, 24½ years, 156 cm. income 600 P.M. Father Class I Gtd. Officer. No bars. Box 21110-CA, Hindustan Times, New Delhi-1.

AN ACADEMICIAN, aged 38, settled in Delhi, would like to meet girls with a view marriage partners. However, the idea behind the ads, the idea of arranging a marriage, is not new in India. The custom of arranged marriages is a longstanding tradition in that country and in many parts of the globe.

ARRANGED MARRIAGES AND LOVE MARRIAGES

Arranged marriages differ from the love marriages that are most common in the United States. Love marriages occur after a couple meets, dates, and "falls in love." Marriage usually follows a period called engagement, and being in love is always considered the most important test of whether to marry. If a man and woman are in love but do not have the approval of parents, they often disregard the parents' wishes. Thus, in the United States marriage follows love.

Arranged marriages in many ways reverse this order. That is, the process could be called one of marriage followed by love. In traditional versions of arranged marriage, the boy or his parents approach the girl's parents about the possibility of marriage. Sometimes a go-between, or matchmaker, brings the two sets of parents together to discuss the marriage of their children. If the parents reach agreement on the match, the wedding date is set and the future bride and groom are informed that they will soon marry. Some past traditions held that the bride and groom should not see each other until the wedding ceremony.

In many parts of Asia and Africa, this older style has given way to modern versions of arranged marriage that allow the boy and girl more choice. Parents and matchmakers still play an important role, however. Parents seek out suitable partners for their children by consulting matchmakers, often neighbors or relatives. In large cities, the role of matchmaker may be filled by newspaper ads or by matrimonial services.

Once parents have found a possible match, they chaperone a first meeting. At this point, the young people may choose to see each other again or to end the association.

Thus they can veto their parents' choice, but they still depend on parents to set up the original meeting. If the couple chooses to continue seeing each other, they might go to the park or zoo, to movies or plays, always with a chaperone. After a few such "dates," wedding arrangements are made.

While this is the general pattern of arranged marriage, specific customs vary. Below are two case studies describing how some marriages are arranged in India and Japan.

INDIA: GEETA AND PURSHOTTAM [1]

Geeta's father and older brothers had been approached several times by families seeking a match for their sons. However, none of the arrangements had worked out, and at age 25, Geeta remained unmarried. Either the boys did not meet the expectations of Geeta's family or else she found them unappealing.

Finally, one of Geeta's brothers suggested that his friend Purshottam might be a good match for Geeta. Her family agreed but spotted one problem. Purshottam's family lived in a traditional joint household, and Geeta might have trouble adjusting to life with them. But when Geeta was asked about the matter, she offered no objection. She trusted her family completely.

Purshottam was approached and showed interest. He decided to marry Geeta. He asked his father for his blessing and participation in the wedding ceremony. Despite some objections his father agreed.

Meanwhile, Geeta's father had been studying Purshottam's horoscope, a guide to his character and future success based on the position of the stars at his birth. Finding nothing in the horoscope which would hinder a marriage, he invited Purshottam's family to tea so that Geeta and Purshottam could be introduced. It was a formal occasion with everyone trying to make a good impression.

After the tea, both families discussed at length the proposed marriage. Geeta liked Purshottam, and her brother knew his character was sound. A message was sent that Geeta's family had agreed to the marriage. A few days later, Geeta received a piece of jewelry from Purshottam's family as a sign they would accept her as his wife.

The many details of planning a wedding were begun by the families. Purshottam sent notes to Geeta and was allowed to take her places. As couples begin to know each other at this stage, they sometimes decide against the match. The wedding can be cancelled with a few hard feelings, but this wedding would not be cancelled.

An engagement ceremony was held a short time before the wedding. Geeta's family brought gifts to Purshottam's family.

Now turning back was more difficult. It would have been considered improper for Geeta to cancel the wedding after the engagement ceremony.

Astrologers were consulted to set the best day and time for the wedding. Finally the day arrived. The wedding was held on a friend's lawn amid colored lights, flowers, tables, chairs, and a platform for the ceremony. Geeta's family arrived first. Purshottam made a traditional bridegroom's entrance on the back of a white mare, leading his family. The families greeted each other warmly, and the ceremony proceeded.

The story of Geeta and Purshottam is typical of middle class city families. Only 20 percent of all Indians live in cities, whereas 80 percent live in rural villages. In rural areas arranged marriages are probably more traditional, and the young people would pobably not have been consulted before the first meeting. Indeed, the first meeting might be at the wedding ceremony. As in Geeta's story, however, the family is trusted completely to find a good match.

Modern Japan is a mixture of tradition and change. Arranged marriages are traditional, but a 1975 survey showed that approximately 60 percent of Japanese marriages today are love marriages. As might be expected, more love marriages were reported in cities than in rural areas. Even so, over 50 percent of the rural couples reported their marriage to be based on love.

Yet the custom of arranged marriage remains strong. Parental guidance in choosing a marriage partner is still valued by many Japanese. One million marriages occur each year in Japan, and 40 percent are arranged. In Japan the divorce rate for these arranged marriages tends to be lower than for love marriages.

JAPAN: MICHIKO AND MORIJI

Moriji chose to let his parents arrange his marriage after he observed the problems faced by his older brother who had married his girlfriend against the wishes of his parents. Many troubles followed, and they were later divorced. Moriji trusted his parents to help him avoid such problems.

The best friend of Moriji's mother agreed to serve as the nakodo—the go-between. She knew that Michiko's family was seeking a good husband for their daughter, and she thought Michiko and Moriji would be very compatible. Matters such as education, health, temperament, and family history were discussed with both families. The astrologer was also consulted. When all signs looked favorable, the *miai*, or first meeting, was agreed to.

A well-known restaurant was chosen for the *miai*. Moriji and Michiko were accompanied by their parents for this important occasion. The conversation was formal, but both the prospective bride and groom were impressed. Either could have ended the matter, and the go-between would have begun reviewing other possibilities.

But neither Moriji nor Michiko wished to break off the arrangement. They exchanged engagement gifts and made wedding plans. The young couple became better acquainted by going to concerts, movies, and museums. Then, seven weeks after the first meeting, they were married.

In recent years, huge numbers of Japanese people have moved to large cities. Arranging a marriage is more difficult in the cities than in the countryside. Because of this, the Japanese have begun to explore other methods of finding possible marriage partners.

For example, the Association of Bridal Counsellors, based in Tokyo, has developed as a type of go-between. Young people seeking matches sometimes turn to counseling offices found in large hotels throughout Japan. There they can review photos and biographies filed by other eligible young people. Some counseling offices videotape interviews with prospective husbands and wives. Over 3,000 such interviews have been recorded. If two young people are impressed with each other's interview, their families arrange a *miai*.

Questions for Discussion

1. What is an arranged marriage? What is a love marriage? Give examples of each.

2. Compare the stories of arranged marriage in India and in Japan. How are the stories similar? How are they different? How would you explain the differences?

A CONVERSATION ON MARRIAGE

Heather: I just find it hard to believe that in India you want your parents to arrange your marriage, Radhika.

Radhika: Well, Heather, it seems strange to me that American girls should want to find their own husbands.

Heather: Does it really? I still can't believe it.

Radhika: Well, don't you find it humiliating to have to attract boys?

Heather: What do you mean?

Radhika: Let me try to explain. As I understand your system in America, getting married depends on whether a girl can attract a boyfriend. She must call attention to herself, using makeup, hairstyles, and the latest fashions to make herself look pretty. If she is shy and doesn't want to do all that, she might end up unmarried.

Heather: Well, don't some women remain unmarried in India?

Radhika: Under arranged marriage, we don't have to worry about that. We know we'll be married. When we reach the proper age, our parents will find a suitable boy. We don't have to compete with other girls or pretend we're better than we are in order to attract a boy. We can simply be ourselves. Trying to make a good impression on boys must truly be humiliating.

Heather: But how can you marry someone if you're not in love with him?

Radhika: We realize that love can blind us and make us ignore problems that will give us much trouble later on. Our parents are older and wiser and better able to choose the right boy. I could easily make a mistake because I am so young. But don't think there is no love in arranged marriage. We expect to fall in love with our husband, and that's what usually happens. An Indian poetess in the thirteenth century explained the way we view our future husband:

> *Without seeing thy face I have given thee a place*
> *in my own eye, like the pupil.*
> *I have only heard thy name and I love thee.*
> *I have not seen thee, and yet I love thee as if I*
> *had seen and known thee.*

Heather: But surely this doesn't always work out. Don't some arranged marriages end in divorce?

Radhika: Well, yes, divorce sometimes occurs. More often, though, if the match is not a good one, people just put up with an unhappy marriage. If the family is poor, they might have no other choice. But surely unhappy marriage is a bigger problem in America. I have read that in your country one out of every three marriages ends in divorce. Many seem to fall "out of love," don't they?

Heather: You're right that divorce affects many people in America. And I see better now why you like arranged marriages. But there is one thing Americans insist on that you do not have in arranged marriage—individual choice. We do not rely on our parents to choose a husband for us. After all, we have to live with him, not our parents. We want to make our own choice, our own decision. Even if it turns out to be an unhappy marriage, we don't wish to give up our right to choose.

Radhika: I see. I am glad to hear your views. I think that choosing a marriage partner shows some interesting differences between our cultures.

Questions

1. What differences between India and the United States are revealed in this conversation? List what was important to Radhika in finding a husband. Then list what was important to Heather and compare the two.

2. How would you answer Radhika's comment that it must be humiliating for girls to try to impress boys? Perhaps she would say the same about boys trying to impress girls. Do American

teen-agers worry about "looking just right" and "making good impressions"?

3. What commercials would *not* be on television if Americans practiced arranged marriages instead of love marriages?

Lesson 6: Apartness

Introduction

Human rights issues have become a vital global concern. Problems of racism, civil rights, sexism, ageism, and religious discrimination have received worldwide attention, especially in the last twenty years. Local, previously isolated events are now broadcast to the world instantaneously, thanks to rapid advances in communications technology. A government's denial of basic human rights can adversely affect that country's relations with other nations.

On a smaller scale, individual publicity about violations of human rights is an increasingly popular method of guaranteeing human rights. Thus it is becoming almost impossible to say, "I didn't know what was happening." Because the guarantee of human rights is even more important in an increasingly interdependent world, an understanding of human rights issues is essential for young people as well as for adults.

This lesson will demonstrate the meaning of discrimination in human terms—first through a simple board game, then through text materials on apartheid in South Africa.

·Objectives

1. Students will be able to draw analogies between their experiences in a board game and the experiences of citizens living under apartheid in South Africa.

2. Students will be able to identify evidence of apartheid in a drawing of a real life situation.

3. Students will be able to give examples of ways the government of South Africa discriminates against nonwhites.

Suggested Procedures

You will need to construct a simple board game, like the one shown on page 57, to accompany this lesson. Make a game board

56

with 32 spaces; each space should be large enough to hold four game markers. One space on the board is marked "Go," and play begins and ends here.

Figure 1

Cut out six game cards each from blue, pink, yellow, and green paper. Each card indicates the number of spaces a player can move on his or her turn. A sample card is shown in Figure 2.

Figure 2

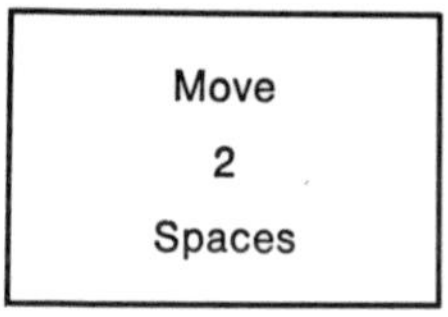

> Move
>
> 2
>
> Spaces

Using the table below, write the following numbers on the cards of each designated color:

Blue cards: 4,5,5,7,7,8   (for a total of 36 spaces)
Pink cards: 3,3,4,4,4,5   (for a total of 23 spaces)
Yellow cards: 3,3,3,4,4,4   (for a total of 21 spaces)
Green cards: 1,1,2,2,3,3   (for a total of 12 spaces)

You might construct matching color markers to indicate each player's position on the board.

If more than four students play each game, divide them into teams. In a large class some students could observe the game, but it is better if many games are going on simultaneously, thereby permitting everyone to play.

The game will be most effective if students are unaware of the topic of the lesson before they begin. Distribute the game boards and cards, then explain the following rules:

1. Place the game cards face down on the board, divided according to color.

2. Each player or team designated as blue, pink, yellow, or green will draw a card from its matching stack to learn how many spaces to move. Moves will be made in the following order: blue first, pink second, yellow third, and green last. Each player will draw a card in turn until all cards are exhausted or until there is a winner, whatever occurs first.

After each group has finished, debrief the players using questions such as:

- Which team won the game?
- Why do you think that team won?
- Is this a fair game? Why or why not?
- If you belonged to a losing team, how did you feel during the game? What could you have done to win the game?
- If you belonged to the winning team, would you have been willing to change the game? How?
- Do you think that this game could represent real conditions somewhere in the world? Where?

Ask students to read the first two paragraphs on apartheid on page 59 and discuss how the game symbolizes apartheid in South Africa. The blue team symbolized whites in South Africa—all the rules were in their favor. The pink and yellow teams represented the Asians and "coloureds." In South Africa these two groups are caught in the middle between blacks and whites; they aspire to reach equality with white South Africans from a separate, unequal position. The green team represented black South Africans, the group that makes the least progress.

Ask students to find evidence of apartheid in the drawing on page 60. You might use the following questions as a guide:

- What is the meaning of the rope? (It divides the seats between white and nonwhite.)
- Is the weather warm or cold? How can you tell? Is everyone

dressed for cool weather? (The weather is cool or cold. The people on the left are dressed warmly—coats, gloves. On the right some people are barefoot, wearing short-sleeved shirts.)
- In what part of the sports stadium are the seats probably located? (Near the end, in the section containing the worst "white" seats and the best "nonwhite" seats. The action is probably off to the left of the picture.)
- Which fans have cameras? (Only the whites.)

Assign pages 61-63 as reading and then lead a class discussion based on the questions on page 63. Remind students that conditions such as these may change rapidly.

The lesson could be extended in several ways. Students might study other examples of "legal discrimination" (such as "Jim Crow" laws) and compare these cases with apartheid. Students could also investigate the current situation in South Africa and analyze whether conditions are changing.

Student Materials

APARTHEID

The game you played in class is based on life as it is today in the Republic of South Africa. The game of "Apartness" is unfair toward the Green, Yellow, and Pink players. The Blue players always win because the game rules favor them. In South Africa, people with white skin are favored over nonwhites. The nonwhites include: (1) blacks, (2) people of mixed racial background, whom white South Africans call "coloureds," and (3) Asians who live in South Africa. This system of rule in South Africa is called *apartheid* (a-par-tite). Apartheid means "apartness"—groups of people are kept apart on the basis of skin color.

In South Africa only white people have the right to vote or hold office in the government. This government over many years has passed laws aimed at keeping people separate according to their skin color. For example, black Africans may own land only in areas called "homelands" scattered around the country. Blacks live in the "homelands" unless they work in the cities.

On the following page is a drawing based on a photograph taken at a sporting event in South Africa. What evidence of apartheid can you find?

Black South Africans who work in the cities are not allowed to stay in the cities after work. Instead they board commuter trains that take them to black communities on the outskirts of the city. The only blacks left in the cities are servants of white families. Nonwhites are not even allowed to visit family members in the cities at night, and this is a great hardship for some families. The decree printed below shows one way the government tries to keep whites separate from nonwhites.

Servants can now have no visitors at night

STAFF REPORTER

NON-WHITE servants in White areas may no longer have visitors between the hours of 10 p.m. and 8 a.m. This was brought into immediate effect yesterday by proclamation in the Government Gazette.

The ban on night-time visitors also includes other Non-Whites permitted to live in White areas in South Africa.

Group Areas Act legislation empowering the **Government** to impose new restrictions on domestic servants was passed by Parliament last year.

The following story is an excerpt from a newspaper article that describes the effect of the decree.[2]

Sarah Makhomola and her husband see each other for about an hour an evening in her backyard room in Saxonwold, Johannesburg. Then he walks the three miles back to his own room and goes to bed.

He has to be on his way by 10 p.m. and cannot return before 8 a.m. The reason is a Government proclamation last weekend that a servant having visitors between those hours is liable to a maximum fine of R400. Or two years. Or both.

Sarah and her husband, Mr. Dickson Hasthu, have been married for 23 years. They have three children—Pauline, 14, Gravis, 16, and Eric, 19.

Sarah usually finishes her work in the kitchen about 8:15 p.m. Sometimes she stays later. At 6 p.m. her husband finishes his work as a gardener and handyman at San Salvador Convent on the corner of First Avenue and Melville Road. He washes, changes, walks to Northwhold Drive, and waits for his wife. It's time for their hour together again.

They can see each other daily. And Sarah gets every second Sunday and one day in the week off. But they cannot see their children unless they go to the children's boarding school in Pietersburg, 209 miles away.

Before the proclamation, Sarah used to have one child at a time visit her during the holidays. It was illegal. They had no permits.

Now, however, Sarah is afraid of more police raids for illegal visitors and has decided not to invite her children to visit her. "They will go to my grandmother near Pietersburg," she said yesterday.

In South Africa there are other laws aimed at keeping nonwhites separate from whites. These include the following:

- A nonwhite African worker is forbidden to take part in a strike for any reason whatsoever.
- Blacks may not work in skilled jobs.
- Nonwhite Africans break the law if they teach friends to read and write free of charge.
- It is unlawful for a white person and a nonwhite person to drink a cup of tea together anywhere in South Africa unless they have a special permit.
- If there is only one waiting room in a railway station, the stationmaster may reserve the room for whites only. If a nonwhite person enters the station, he or she is guilty of a criminal offense.

- Black parents must pay for their child's education. Education for white children is free.

Study the following chart. According to this chart, who seems to benefit from these laws?

Population and Income in South Africa by Groups

Groups	Population	Income
Whites	18%	73%
Blacks	68%	19%
Asians and Coloureds	14%	8%

South Africa is a nation rich in natural resources and manufacturing. Gold, asbestos, copper, platinum, manganese, iron, sugar, coal, grain, wool, and most of the world's diamonds are found there. But whites are the sole owners of that country's industries. The average income among whites is over ten times the combined income of blacks, Asians, and "coloureds." Whites also receive up to ten times more pay for doing exactly the same jobs as nonwhites.

In South Africa people are discriminated against on the basis of their skin color. White South Africans claim that they arrived in the country first, so blacks have no rights; however, there is little historical evidence for this claim. A more likely reason for apartheid is fear of competition. Four times as many blacks as whites live in South Africa, and many whites feel the only way they can remain in control is to legally prevent blacks from gaining economic or political power.

Discussion Questions

1. Why do you think the South African government tries to to keep whites separate from nonwhites?

2. What did the decree on page 61 mean to Sarah Makhomola, her husband, and children?

3. What would the laws on pages 62-63 probably mean to you if you were a nonwhite living in South Africa? What would they mean to you if you were a white living there?

3. Evaluation in Global Studies

Teachers who wish to add a global studies dimension to their instruction must recognize the need to evaluate this new approach. Two aspects of evaluation are discussed in this chapter: *program evaluation*, determining whether the school curriculum provides students with a comprehensive understanding of global concerns; and *student evaluation*, judging whether students are achieving instructional objectives in global studies.

Program Evaluation

Establishing Program Objectives

Program objectives, or curriculum goals, are broad statements of intentions. Some examples of program objectives for a global studies program are found in a 1976 publication of the Center for Global Perspectives:[1]

1. To provide students with the ability to perceive all individuals as members of a single species of life
2. To provide students with the ability to perceive all humans as a part of the earth's biosphere
3. To provide students with the ability to see how each person and each group participates in the world's sociocultural system

4. To provide students with the ability to perceive all people as both "culture borrowers" and "culture depositors"

5. To provide students with the ability to perceive that people have differing perceptions, beliefs, and attitudes about the world system.

Such examples indicate a format for program objectives, but they barely suggest the range of possible outcomes. In order to be certain that their school has considered a broad range of objectives, teachers might find a checklist helpful.

The checklist of program objectives described in this chapter focuses on three dimensions: "global-local interconnections," "area studies," and "planet-wide concerns." Global-local interconnections refer to ways local communities are linked to the global system. Contacts include imports, exports, travel, education, business, and religion. A project called "Columbus in the World: The World in Columbus," directed by Chadwick Alger at Ohio State University, found that the city of Columbus, Ohio had extensive global contacts through international travelers, foreign students, multinational corporations, business activities, church activities, international artists, and so on. In effect, each segment of this midwestern city had its own "foreign policy," a policy guiding relationships within the global system.

Since the Columbus project, some school systems have tried to assess global-local interconnections in their own communities. Suggestions on how to gather material in your own community can be found in Chapter 4.

A second dimension of program objectives is area studies—the study of a single region or area of the world, such as East Asia, South Asia, the Middle East, Africa, Latin America, Western Europe, Eastern Europe, and Australia. Typically, the area studies approach includes a study of the language, politics, history, geography, arts, and economy of a region. By studying one region at a time, teachers hope that students will understand each culture thoroughly.

A third dimension of program objectives is termed planet-wide concerns. This refers to a study of basic human concerns that touch everyone the world over—food, health, energy, work, the family, communication, human rights, peace, education, transportation, the arts. This approach, used by the Global Studies Project at Indiana University, treats each topic as a basic and universal human activity, drawing attention both to shared characteristics and to unique, culturally conditioned features.

A global perspective is different from the area studies approach in that area studies treats each world region as a whole, one at a time. A study of India might cover such food topics as diet, agriculture, and food taboos. Later, the same food topics might be examined for Africa, and still later for Western Europe. A global perspective raises the level of analysis to the planet level. Food issues are compared and contrasted as they appear in human experience, not studied as they occur country by country. The global perspective implies a broad "spaceship earth" view of human phenomena.

How to Use the Checklist

A checklist can be used to determine the quality and scope of your school's global studies program. The checklist included here appears in three sections, geared to the three "dimensions" described above. For each section the topics on the left indicate the range of topics included in exemplary programs. These topics might be covered in one or more of the school subjects listed across the top of each checklist.

To determine the scope of global studies in your curriculum, the evaluator should write the number of the grade (K-12) in any box, indicating where topics are included in program objectives for that grade level. Grade-level numbers imply that the curriculum includes objectives on that topic for that grade level. For the most accurate, up-to-date evaluation, ask teachers at each grade level to complete the checklist.

This checklist can also be used to determine the quality of the global studies program. After making grade-level notations, the evaluator can use a symbol to indicate the quality of treatment given to each topic:

$++$ program quality is exemplary on this topic
$+$ program quality is high on this topic
$\sqrt{}$ program quality is adequate on this topic
$-$ program quality is low on this topic
$--$ program quality is very low on this topic

This system permits a distinction between program coverage and program quality. Your school curriculum may cover all the topics on the checklist, but quality of treatment may be brief and superficial.

GLOBAL STUDIES PROGRAM EVALUATION CHECKLIST

Directions: The left column lists topics that represent program objectives in global studies. Mark the grade(s) (K-12) in the box under the subject where that objective is taught. Then to assess quality of the program, mark one of the following symbols after each number entered:

++   program quality is exemplary on this topic
+   program quality is high on this topic
√   program quality is adequate on this topic
—   program quality is low on this topic
—— program quality is very low on this topic

I. GLOBAL-LOCAL INTERCONNECTIONS: Studying the World from a Local Perspective

	Social Studies	Language Arts	Math	Science	Foreign Language	Music	Art	Industrial Arts	Home Economics	Health/Safety	Driver Education
A. Imported products/ideas											
B. Exported products/ideas											
C. Global-local business connections											
D. Global-local transportation connections											
E. Global-local education connections											
F. Global-local arts connections											
G. Global-local language connections											
H. Global-local family heritage connections											
I. Global-local media connections											

II. AREA STUDIES: Studying the World from a National/Regional Perspective

	Social Studies	Language Arts	Math	Science	Foreign Language	Music	Art	Industrial Arts	Home Economics	Health/Safety	Driver Education
A. East Asia											
B. Southeast Asia											
C. South Asia											
D. Australia											
E. Pacific Islands											
F. Middle East											
G. North Africa											
H. East Africa											
I. West Africa											
J. South Africa											
K. West Europe											
L. Scandinavia											
M. East Europe											
N. Soviet Union											
O. Latin America											
P. North America											

III. PLANET-WIDE CONCERNS: Studying the World from a Global Perspective

	Social Studies	Language Arts	Math	Science	Foreign Language	Music	Art	Industrial Arts	Home Economics	Health/Safety	Driver Education
A. Food											
B. Energy											
C. Work											
D. Families											
E. Communication											
F. Human Rights											
G. Peace											
H. Education											
I. Transportation											
J. Pollution											
K. Resources											
L. Wildlife											
M. Arts											
N. Alternative Futures											

Student Evaluation

Establishing Student Objectives

The National Council for the Social Studies recommends instructional objectives in four domains: knowledge, abilities, valuing, and social participation.[2] Global studies objectives can be developed for each area. For example, from the Global Studies Project's unit on families:

1. *Knowledge*—Students can define and give examples of arranged marriages and love marriages.
2. *Abilities*—Students can compare arranged marriage customs in India and in Japan, pointing out similarities and differences between the two nations.

69

3. *Valuing*—Students can make judgments about whether they approve or disapprove of possible future conditions of family life.
4. *Social Participation*—Students can arrange and conduct a discussion with an elderly neighbor or relative about social security and other concerns.

Such objectives are most appropriately called "instructional objectives," rather than "performance objectives." They describe what students are expected to do, but they do not state precisely the two necessary aspects of performance objectives: learning conditions and expected level of mastery. When making a performance evaluation, a teacher must merely decide: Did the student reach the desired level or not? However, performance objectives are not the best tools for this kind of evaluation because they are inappropriate for some objectives (e.g., valuing) and because they require considerable time to prepare. In the absence of specific performance objectives, how does one proceed with evaluation? Some suggestions follow for judging instructional objectives related to knowledge, abilities, valuing, and social participation.

Knowledge

There is no validated norm-referenced test to assess knowledge in global studies. Most often, projects like the Global Studies Project write their own test items. This is one option open to any school district wishing to evaluate student knowledge.

Teachers may also wish to use informal techniques like student interviews, anecdotal logs, written observations, and checklists to measure knowledge in this area. These techniques can be used to evaluate all four types of objectives, but are especially important for the valuing objectives.

Abilities

Abilities or skill objectives as related to global studies have close ties to general social studies skill objectives, such as judging the quality of information sources or assessing the biases of authors and cartoonists. Unfortunately, no formal tests exist, and there is a clear need to develop instruments that can be used to evaluate global studies skills.

One solution is to build a skills checklist based on a general list of skill objectives. Teachers might rate students through observations of discussions, group work, and role-playing activities. Either a simple check-no check system or a more complex rating scheme could be used to assess progress in each skill objective.

Valuing

Valuing objectives, including attitudes, may be measured by questionnaire or observation. Several attitude questionnaires exist, although none is available commercially. Some scales aim at assessing "world mindedness;" others probe attitudes toward specific foreign nations.[3]

Apart from attitude questionnaires, teachers have other ways for assessing valuing objectives. Values and attitudes are expressed daily in the course of classroom discussion, and anecdotal records of teacher observations can be maintained to record student growth and change. A short personal interview with each student can be informative and is likely to elicit candid and honest responses. Some appropriate questions might include:

1. How do you like studying other peoples of the world?
2. Would you like to travel? If so, where?
3. Would you like to learn another language? If so, which one?
4. How do you feel about people in India? in China? in Europe? in Africa? in Latin America?
5. How do you feel about the United Nations?

Responses would not have to be recorded to judge the overall positive or negative character of student attitudes toward the world system. However, maintaining a record of responses, in the form of written notes or symbols on a checklist, allows teachers to judge a student's progress, and such records facilitate a study of an entire classroom or school to determine general student attitudes on global issues.

Social Participation

Objectives for social participation are the least common of the four types discussed. Opportunities for participation in global objectives are greater in some communities than in others. Nevertheless, participation on some level is possible in nearly every community. Evaluation of participation objectives can be completed using a simple checklist such as the following:

Participation Objective

	Sept.	Oct.	Nov.	Dec.	Jan.	Feb.	Mar.	Apr.	May
Work for UNICEF drive									
Visit foreign consulate									
Organize an international fair at your school									
Interview foreign student									
Organize a public debate on a global concern									
Sponsor a performance by an international artist at your school									
Visit a multinational corporation									
Present a global concern to the student council									
Organize a pen pal project with a school in another nation									

Of course, other appropriate activities can be added to such a checklist. The checklist itself could be filled out by students as a self-evaluation, or completed by teachers as they observe student activities over the year.

In summary, evaluation of student objectives in global studies programs can focus on knowledge, skills, values, and participation. The instruments and techniques vary with the type of objective being assessed. Unfortunately, there are no readily available, published instruments for evaluation in global studies. There are instruments, however, that have been developed by research projects to assess knowledge and attitudes. In addition, a variety of locally developed techniques—student interviews, teacher observation checklists, student self-reports, and anecdotal logs—can be used to evaluate student progress on locally adopted global studies objectives.

72

4. Resources for Global Studies

Few textbooks are devoted specifically to global studies. Increased demand for global studies will bring a proportional increase in the quantity and quality of published materials. In the meantime, teachers must find ways to adapt existing materials to global studies purposes.

Rich but often overlooked resources are within reach of a great majority of teachers. Nearly every community contains people and organizations active in global society and willing to share their knowledge and experience. Moreover, many state, national, and international organizations provide free or inexpensive material.

This chapter helps teachers identify global studies resources in three ways: (1) a brief, annotated list of groups and organizations that can provide information about global studies, (2) an "inventory" teachers might employ in the process of identifying resources in their own communities, and (3) a "checklist" to evaluate the global studies content of instructional materials.

Some Sources of Information on Global Studies

Many organizations provide materials that can be used for instruction in global studies. A complete, annotated list would require more space than is available. What follows might be viewed as a "starter list" for teachers beginning to work in this field. Contacts with the sources noted below will lead to further sources of information.

General Publications

Several professional educational organizations have published overviews of global studies that are useful to teachers. The January 1978 *Curriculum Report* (vol. 7, no. 3) of the National Association of Secondary School Principals, entitled "Global Education: A Curriculum Imperative," contains a brief rationale for teaching global studies, describes a few global studies centers, and surveys exemplary school programs. The *Curriculum Report* is available from NASSP, 1904 Association Drive, Reston, Virginia 22091 (50¢ singly, or 30¢ each for 2-10 copies).

The Association for Supervision and Curriculum Development, 1701 K Street, N.W., Suite 1100, Washington, D.C. 20006 has published *Global Studies: Problems and Promises for Elementary Teachers,* a booklet edited by Norman V. Overly and Richard D. Kimpston. This booklet includes chapters on perspectives and approaches to teaching global topics and issues and has an extensive bibliography of resources for elementary school teachers. The booklet is available from ASCD ($4.50).

The January 1977 issue of *Social Education* (vol. 41, no. 1), a publication of the National Council for the Social Studies, is devoted to "Global Education: Adding a New Dimension to Social Studies." This issue, containing eight timely articles, including a section on global education in elementary schools and a selected bibliography, can be ordered from NCSS, Suite 400, 2030 M Street, N.W., Washington, D.C. 20036 ($3.00).

Number 28 in Phi Delta Kappa's fastback series is *Education for a Global Society* by James Becker. Topics include "The Imperatives of Globalism," "Transnational Participation," and "Global Education: Unity and Diversity." The fastback may be ordered from Phi Delta Kappa, Eighth and Union, Box 789, Bloomington, Indiana 47401 (50¢ for members of PDK, 75¢ for nonmembers).

Education for a World in Change: A Working Handbook for Global Perspectives, by David C. King, Margaret S. Branson, and Larry Condon, is published by the Center for Global Perspectives, 218 East 18th Street, New York, New York 10003 ($3.50). This handbook stresses four major concepts—interdependence, conflict, communication, and change—and provides

74

63 pages of sample lessons intended for use at all grade levels.

A few state departments of education have begun to develop guidelines for global education. One, the Michigan Department of Education, Box 30008, Lansing, Michigan 48909, has published a set of guidelines and a bibliography useful to teachers in Michigan and elsewhere.

Global Studies Organizations

The Center for Global Perspectives, mentioned above, offers a wide range of services to teachers, including publications such as *Intercom*, a journal that emphasizes practical teaching suggestions. The subscription rate for *Intercom* is $6/1 year, $11/2 years, or $15/3 years. In the past the Center has produced teacher aids, position papers, and multimedia packages. Its publications list is available without charge.

The Mid-America Program for Global Perspectives in Education works with schools and a variety of civic and educational groups to improve global education, especially in the Midwest. MAP has also produced classroom units and resource guides that are available free or at nominal cost. Write to MAP at 513 North Park Avenue, Indiana University, Bloomington, Indiana 47405.

The Global Development Studies Institute, P.O. Box 522, 14 Main Street, Madison, New Jersey 07940, provides detailed curriculum outlines for secondary schools and undergraduate colleges. An annual subscription to *Memos*, a newsletter that annotates materials relevant to global studies, is $2.50.

The United Nations and its affiliated agencies are especially rich sources of information. Slides, filmstrips, teacher's kits, and display materials can be ordered from the U.S. Committee for UNICEF, The United Nations Children's Fund, 331 East 38th Street, New York, New York 10016. Its catalogue of publications and educational materials is free. Also, the United Nations Association of the U.S.A., a nonprofit, independent organization, publishes a monthly newspaper, *The Interdependent*, that treats global issues and events. A one-year trial subscription is $5.00 from *The Interdependent*, 345 East 46th Street, New York, New York 10017. The UNA also publishes *Helping Boys and Girls Discover the World*, a useful handbook of practical suggestions, promising practices, and specific resources. Write to Publications, 300 East 42nd Street, New York, New York 10017 ($2.50). *The Yearbook of the United Nations*, available in libraries, surveys U.N. activities and has bibliographies on subjects discussed during the year.

Catalogs, Guides, and Directories of Organizations

Educational Resources Information Center (ERIC), a national clearinghouse of information, lists many entries relating to global studies. For a free pamphlet entitled *How To Use ERIC* and a basic bibliography for *International, Intercultural Communication*, write the Speech Communication Association, 5205 Leesburg Pike, Falls Church, Virginia 22041.

The American Library Association publishes a directory of media catalogs entitled *Guides to Educational Media*. One entry is a pamphlet entitled, *Meet Some of Your Four Billion Neighbors at a Film Festival: One Phase of the Project Neighbors Unlimited*, published by the Association for Childhood Education International, 3615 Wisconsin Avenue, N.W., Washington, D.C. 20016 (50¢). This pamphlet lists the addresses, producers, and distributors of a number of global studies films for elementary school children. *Guides to Educational Media* may be found in a library or may be purchased from the ALA, 50 East Huron Street, Chicago, Illinois 60611 ($5.00).

NASA films such as *Images of Life* and *Pollution Solution?* are listed in the *NASA Films* catalog, available free from the National Aeronautics and Space Administration, Washington, D.C. 20546.

Another useful catalog is published by Social Studies School Service, 10000 Culver Boulevard, P.O. Box 802, Culver City, California 90230 and lists over 200 pages of social studies paperbacks, filmstrips, duplicating masters, simulation games, and other items useful in a global studies classroom.

Teachers will find two special directories of particular use in global studies. *A Preliminary Directory of Organizations and Publications for Peace and World Order Educators*, lists and codes 139 organizations and lists of publications. It is available without charge from Transnational Academic Program, Institute for World Order, 1140 Avenue of the Americas, New York, New York 10036. *Directory of Resources in Global Education* describes 83 organizations according to focus, topics, services, publications, and so on. It is available from the Overseas Development Council, Attn: Jayne Millar Wood, 1717 Massachusetts Avenue, N.W., Suite 501, Washington, D.C. 20036 ($2.50).

Locating Global Studies Resources in the Local Community

A number of schools have researched the extent to which their own communities are actively engaged in global society. Students are usually surprised to learn that so many people have traveled abroad or are engaged in some form of transnational interaction.[1]

The first step is to conduct an "inventory" of a community. The inventory can lead to a classroom directory of people, organizations, collections, and other resources that can be tapped for information on global issues. The following checklist is intended to help teachers and students gather the kinds of data they might want for their directory.

INVENTORY OF GLOBAL MATERIALS AND RESOURCES IN THE SCHOOL AND COMMUNITY

Use this checklist to identify possible global studies resources:

(check)

——————— the school library, resource room, media center, or center for materials

——————— parents and community members who may have global knowledge or interests based upon traveling, living, or working abroad

——————— fellow teachers and students who may have global knowledge or interests

——————— local businesses that have international connections

——————— local restaurants that serve international cuisine

——————— local stores that sell international products (grocery stores or gift shops, for example)

——————— the local library

——————— a nearby museum

——————— religious organizations with overseas mission or outreach activities

_____ newspaper accounts of global trends and international affairs

_____ local chapters of international organizations (Rotary, 4-H, Red Cross, etc.)

_____ international exchange and foreign study programs

_____ performing groups (dance, music, drama, athletics)

_____ nearby landmarks where there has been a point of international contact

_____ ethnic neighborhoods

_____ multiple languages spoken locally

_____ local traditions that have an international origin

_____ local events that have global implications

_____ the home (foreign-made products, toys)

_____ television (*The Global Papers, Big Blue Marble,* news specials)

Evaluating Materials for Classroom Use

The following form can help teachers and curriculum committees assess classroom materials. The checklist follows a two-step format. Two rating scales are given for each question, one to judge the merit of the materials under scrutiny and another to judge the merit of the question itself. This two-step method permits evaluators to focus on those aspects of global studies they believe to be most important. Moreover, the task of evaluating materials can also serve the purpose of building consensus within a school about the aims of global education.[2]

A CHECKLIST FOR EVALUATING GLOBAL STUDIES CURRICULUM MATERIALS FOR CLASSROOM USE[3]

Title of materials _____

Copyright date _____

Author(s)/Developer(s) _____

Publisher _____

Format (textbook, filmstrip, etc.) _____

Evaluator _____

What are the intended objectives of the class, unit, or course in which these materials might be used? _____

_____

_____

What are the expressed or implied objectives of these materials?

_____

_____

Is there agreement between the objectives of the materials and the objectives of the class, unit, or course? If not, how do you justify the possible use of these materials? _____

_____

_____

Directions: Answer the following questions by circling a number for each of the two rating scales. The first scale is used to rate the materials being evaluated. The second scale rates the importance of the question itself. In the following example, an evaluator has judged that the title of a set of materials is fairly indicative of the content of the materials, but considered the question itself not important/not applicable. For each question, there is a place to check "see narrative." At the end of the form, there is space to amplify your response.

Sample:

To what extent does the title indicate the content of the materials?

0	1	(2)	3	4
no extent				great extent

This question is:

(0)	1	2	3	4
not applicable/ not important				applicable and extremely important

1. To what extent do the materials emphasize that each person has a unique perspective on the world that may not be shared by others?

   0   1   2   3   4
   no extent   great extent

   This question is:

   0   1   2   3   4
   not applicable/   applicable and
   not important   extremely important

   _____ See narrative

2. To what extent do the materials help students understand that the way we perceive ourselves and other persons influences how we behave toward others?

   0   1   2   3   4
   no extent   great extent

   This question is:

   0   1   2   3   4
   not applicable/   applicable and
   not important   extremely important

   _____ See narrative

3. To what extent do the materials emphasize that there are basic needs, concerns, activities, and rights common to humanity?

   0   1   2   3   4
   no extent   great extent

   This question is:

   0   1   2   3   4
   not applicable/   applicable and
   not important   extremely important

   _____ See narrative

4. To what extent do the materials encourage students to imagine what it would be like to live the life of persons in foreign cultures?

   0   1   2   3   4
   no extent   great extent

   This question is:

   0   1   2   3   4
   not applicable/   applicable and
   not important   extremely important

   _____ See narrative

5. To what extent do the materials develop understanding of concepts such as "change," "growth," "ecology," "system," and "interdependence"?

   0   1   2   3   4
   no extent   great extent

   This question is:

   0   1   2   3   4
   not applicable/   applicable and
   not important   extremely important

   _____ See narrative

6. To what extent do the materials build awareness of current trends and developments that are affecting the world as a whole now and in the future?

   0   1   2   3   4
   no extent   great extent

   This question is:

   0   1   2   3   4
   not applicable/   applicable and
   not important   extremely important

   _____ See narrative

7. To what extent do the materials facilitate the analysis of problems such as overpopulation, pollution, poverty, racism, and war?

   0   1   2   3   4
   no extent   great extent

   This question is:

   0   1   2   3   4
   not applicable/   applicable and
   not important   extremely important

   _____ See narrative

8. To what extent do the materials foster an understanding of how human organizations such as governments, churches, and corporations interact globally?

   0   1   2   3   4
   no extent   great extent

   This question is:

   0   1   2   3   4
   not applicable/   applicable and
   not important   extremely important

   _____ See narrative

9. To what extent do the materials give recognition to the fact that the world's wealth is unequally distributed?

0   1   2   3   4
no extent   great extent

This question is:

0   1   2   3   4
not applicable/   applicable and
not important   extremely important

_____ See narrative

10. To what extent do the materials give recognition to the fact that the world's resources are finite and limited?

0   1   2   3   4
no extent   great extent

This question is:

0   1   2   3   4
not applicable/   applicable and
not important   extremely important

_____ See narrative

11. To what extent do the materials develop an understanding of how one's personal choices can affect others around the world?

0   1   2   3   4
no extent   great extent

This question is:

0   1   2   3   4
not applicable/   applicable and
not important   extremely important

_____ See narrative

12. To what extent do the materials help students to make comparisons and look for interrelationships across cultures, nations, or subgroups of societies?

0   1   2   3   4
no extent   great extent

This question is:

0   1   2   3   4
not applicable/   applicable and
not important   extremely important

_____ See narrative

13. To what extent do the materials encourage the appreciation of individual and group differences around the world?

0	1	2	3	4
no extent				great extent

This question is:

0	1	2	3	4
not applicable/ not important				applicable and extremely important

_____ See narrative

14. To what extent do the materials encourage speculating, forecasting, scenario writing, and other ways of estimating how the world may be in the future?

0	1	2	3	4
no extent				great extent

This question is:

0	1	2	3	4
not applicable/ not important				applicable and extremely important

_____ See narrative

15. To what extent do the materials inspire students to see that all persons are members of one global family as well as members of localities, cultures, and nations?

0	1	2	3	4
no extent				great extent

This question is:

0	1	2	3	4
not applicable/ not important				applicable and extremely important

_____ See narrative

Conclusions

16. To what extent are the materials generally teachable?

0	1	2	3	4
no extent				great extent

This question is:

0	1	2	3	4
not applicable/ not important				applicable and extremely important

_____ See narrative

17. To what extent are the materials generally learnable?

0	1	2	3	4
no extent				great extent

This question is:

0	1	2	3	4
not applicable/ not important				applicable and extremely important

_____ See narrative

18. To what extent are the materials suitable for students with special learning needs?

0	1	2	3	4
no extent				great extent

This question is:

0	1	2	3	4
not applicable/ not important				applicable and extremely important

_____ See narrative

19. To what extent are the materials packaged in a suitable format?

0	1	2	3	4
no extent				great extent

This question is:

0	1	2	3	4
not applicable/ not important				applicable and extremely important

_____ See narrative

20. To what extent do you recommend that these materials be purchased or used?

0	1	2	3	4
no extent				great extent

Narrative Section

Question number _____

Comments:

Question number _____

Comments:

84

References

References

Chapter One—Rationale for Global Studies

1. C. E. Black, *The Dynamics of Modernization: A Study of Comparative History* (New York: Harper & Row, 1966).
2. Donald Kendall, *Industry Week* (May 14, 1978).
3. Norman Cousins, "Need: A New World Theme Song," *Saturday Review* (July 1968).
4. The classification of problems draws upon a formulation found in Joseph Campbell, and others, *Changing Images of Man* (Menlo Park, California: Stanford Research Institute, 1974).
5. Judith V. Torney, "The International Attitudes and Knowledge of Adolescents in Nine Countries: The IEA Civic Education Survey," *International Journal of Political Education* (September 1977): 3-20.
6. An additional curricular response is found at Stevenson High School in Livonia, Michigan, where students are offered the option of an alternative to the regular school through a multidisciplinary school-within-a-school teaching social studies, English, science, mathematics, and Spanish.

Chapter Two—Lessons for Global Studies

1. This story is adapted from Margaret Anne Sood, *The Urban Middle Class Family in India* (New Delhi: Education Resources Center, 1974).
2. Peter Wellman, "Separated By the New Decree," *Rand Daily Mail*, March 21, 1970.

Chapter Three—Evaluation in Global Studies

1. See *Intercom*, no. 84/85 (1976); for additional global studies objectives consult Jon Kinghorn, *Implementation Guide to School Improvement Through Global Education* (Dayton, Ohio: Charles F. Kettering Foundation, 1978).
2. NCSS guidelines for social studies can be found in *Social Education* 35, no. 8 (December 1971): 853-869.
3. See, for example, the "world-mindedness scale" developed by Donald Sampson and Howard Smith, "A Scale to Measure World-Minded Attitudes," *Journal of Social Psychology* 45 (1975): 99-106; Charles Mitsakos, "An Examination of the Effect of the 'Family of Man' Social Studies Program on Third-Grade Children's Views of Foreign People" (unpublished doctoral dissertation, Boston University, 1977); "Global Mindedness Scale for Youth," Charles F. Kettering Foundation, 1975; and Victor Smith, "The Effects of a Global Studies Course on the International Attitudes of Junior High School Students" (unpublished doctoral dissertation, Indiana University, 1977).

Chapter Four—Resources for Global Studies

1. Some suggestions for taking instructional advantage of local resources can be found in Charlotte C. Anderson and Barbara J. Winston, "Membership in a Global Society: Implications and Instructional Strategies," *Journal of Geography* 76 (January 1977): 18-23.
2. The notion of improving schools by conducting school self-evaluation exercises and "we agree" workshops is being developed by the North Central Association and the Charles F. Kettering Foundation. The *Handbook for Global Education: A Working Manual* by Jon Rye Kinghorn and William P. Shaw is available from the Charles F. Kettering Foundation, Suite 300, 5335 Far Hills Avenue, Dayton, Ohio 45429.
3. The idea for this checklist is based upon a scheme developed by the Indiana State Department of Public Instruction for use in reviewing textbooks offered for state adoption.

4271